The Marque Has Returned

The MG RV8 is a special edition of 2,000 cars, and went on sale in the spring of 1993.

For further product information, and details of availability, write to
Rover Cars UK Operations, P.O. Box 395, Longbridge, Birmingham B31 2TB.

FROM SUCCESS TO SUCCESS...

Congratulations to the MGB V8
HAPPY 21st BIRTHDAY

From the Haymarket Motoring Titles

60 Waldegrave Road
Teddington
Middlesex TW11 8LG

Tel: 081 943 5000

38-42 Hampton Road
Teddington
Middlesex TW11 0JE

MG V8

Foreword

By John Towers

It is widely recognised that the Rover Group has successfully implemented a radical change in its business and product strategy over the past few years.

From a tenuous existence as a volume manufacturer, Rover has re-focused, and is proving progressively that there is a place in the markets of Europe — and further afield — for a product range which offers a distinctive image, prestige and refinement.

A key aspect of that progress is the reputation of British motor vehicle craftsmanship. While the Rover name itself reflects world-renowned traditions, the MG marque represents an equally illustrious pedigree.

Rover was consequently both proud and delighted to mark the thirtieth anniversary of the MGB by announcing the MG RV8 at the British International Motor Show in 1992. Though it is a modern version of the most famous and successful MG in history — a retrospective rather than a view of the future — the MG RV8 has rapidly generated intense international interest. And that enthusiasm will be an important factor in helping Rover to decide on any future plans for sports car development and manufacture.

This carefully researched and evocative book is a timely reminder of the evolution of the original Abingdon-built MGB — the MGB GT V8 — and also a celebration of the birth of its spiritual successor.

John Towers

MANAGING DIRECTOR, ROVER GROUP

MG V8

Twenty-One Years On. . .
From Introduction to RV8

David Knowles
and the MG Car Club V8 Register

Windrow
&
Greene
AUTOMOTIVE

Published in Great Britain by
Windrow & Greene Ltd
19A Floral Street
London WC2E 9DS

© David Knowles, 1994

A C.I.P. catalogue record for this book
is available from the British Library.

ISBN I 872004 89 X

Designed by:
ghk DESIGN, Chiswick, London

Printed in
Great Britain

Acknowledgements

*No book can be produced without a great deal of help from others, and the
present volume is no exception. I would like, therefore, gratefully to
acknowledge the help of the following people, without whom this book would
not have been possible:*

Particular thanks must of course go to my co-authors, Roger Parker, Geoff Allen and
Dave Wellings. Thanks are also due to: Liz English, of Haymarket Archives; Michael
Kennedy, Denis Chick, Kevin Jones, Brian Newell, Leanne Evans, Alex Stephenson,
Mike Trazinski, Dave Peers, Mike O'Hara, John Yea, Don Wyatt, Simon Maris, Graham
Irvine, Mark Gamble and Cliff Law, of the Rover Group; Ian Elliott, former Rover
Product Affairs Manager; David Bishop, Jack Bellinger, David Bloomfield, Anders
Clausager, Karam Ram, Rex Trueman and Peter Mitchell, of British Motor Heritage;
Richard Lamb, of *What Car?*; John Uden and Bernie Simmonds, of English Heritage, for
permission to use the grounds of Chiswick House for the front cover; John Thornley,
Terry Mitchell, Don Hayter, Mike Allison, Jim O'Neill, the late Roy Brocklehurst, Brian
Hillier, Cliff Bray, Basil Smith, Bob Neville, all former MG personnel; David Wall,
ex-Rover, Solihull; Colin Walkey, Land Rover; Ken Costello; Ron Gammons; Ron
Armstrong, Merie Sharman, Keith Rowson, Clive Wheatley, MG Car Club V8 Register
Committee members; Brian Halford, Rod Longton, Neville Marriner, BCV8
Championship; John Heagren, V8 Concours Champion; *Car* magazine; Robin Dodson,
Tom Studer, Bas Geritts, Gerhard Maier, Brian Field, Steve Cox, Mike Dunlop, Philip
Armitage, Roger Righini, who own the pre-production, lhd and ex-Press Demonstrator
MGB GT V8s featured; Peter Rushforth; Messrs. Foster & Skerrington; Graham Smith;
Mark Vine; Chris Goffey; Ken Smith; Lothar Taverne; Brian Hutchings; Len Cross, for
the front cover photograph; Andy Williams (not the singer!); Dave Vale; Roger Cook;
James Taylor; Graham Robson; Malcolm Green; Harry Webster; David Hadden;
Windrow & Greene, my publishers, for their faith in me; and many others who have
been generous with both time and material. Special thanks are also due to the specialist
advertisers in this book. Last, but not least, I must acknowledge my debt of gratitude
to my wife Shirley and daughters Katie and Emily, all of whom have patiently and
graciously supported me during the whole exercise!

FRONT COVER, MAIN PHOTOGRAPH
*The front cover features the author's own 1974
Damask Red MGB GT V8, together with a
Woodcote Green MG RV8 Press Demonstrator
car. The cars are pictured in the attractive
setting of the forecourt of Chiswick House, the
style of which was inspired by the 16th century
architect, Palladio. Chiswick House was built for
Lord Burlington in 1725-9, and is now cared for
by English Heritage, by whose kind permission it
was used as a location.*

*The MG badge and octagon are registered
trademarks and are used by kind permission
of the Rover Group.*

Contents

Introduction

by Ron Armstrong

Chairman, MG Car Club V8 Register, 1990-1994

I count it as a real honour to be asked to write this introduction but, at the same time, I feel that it is the least I can do to repay the debt I owe to the MG V8 for the pleasure it has given me for the last seven years. This book celebrates the twenty-first anniversary of the MGB GT V8, launched, in August 1973, into a world where heated rear windscreens and tinted glass were still something of a novelty. In those far-off days (which some of us remember well!) the impact and reputation of the GT V8 in the market place was solid but not spectacular. In the 1990s, however, the car has matured into a sought-after classic with a much-admired character, based largely upon its wonderful engine, which has endeared it to many happy owners and has led to a growing number of superb MGB V8 conversions.

I very much hope that readers enjoy this book, ably written and assembled by David Knowles and with a host of material contributed by V8 experts and enthusiasts: never before have the members of the MG V8 clan got together in this way to honour their favourite car.

A fortunate few are already driving examples of the direct descendant of the MGB GT V8, the new MG RV8. We are delighted that the Rover Group has not only kept the MG marque alive but has done so in the shape of the spiritual successor to the original.

So the V8 theme is very much alive and kicking, not only in the form of the many immaculate V8s which one sees at gatherings and on the race circuits throughout the year but also in the new MG shape on the roads of the UK. Long may it continue to thrive!

Ron Armstrong

Watford, Herts.
January 1994

The MG Heritage

Origins

The MG marque is renowned the world over for the most successful series of small sports cars ever built. Few other marques can boast such an enthusiastic following or such a long and distinguished history. Thriving MG clubs are to be found in all corners of the globe and the host of companies involved in restoring, maintaining and modifying MGs, or providing the means to do so, would be impossible to count.

Virtually all the great classic marques, such as Bentley, Bugatti, Jaguar, Lancia and others, have been dominated by individuals of outstanding talent and flair, and MG is no exception.

Its origins lie in a business established by William Morris (later Lord Nuffield) which began by selling and repairing bicycles and went on, within an astonishingly short space of time, to racing thoroughbred sports cars in some of the greatest races in the world. At the head of this enterprise was Cecil Kimber, appointed by Morris originally as Sales Manager for Morris Garages, but soon to become the General Manager, following the death of the previous incumbent

Unlike many of the industry's legendary figures, Cecil Kimber was no great engineer. But he undoubtedly had a flair for styling and he knew what the customer wanted; he was personally responsible for the lines of the classic 1930s MGs. Kimber knew precisely where his strengths lay, and he was able to draw around him an able-bodied group of loyal staff, the like of which has seldom been seen in the history of any other motor manufacturer. It is Kimber we should thank for establishing the style of the marque, and it is the gifted men who gave so many productive years to the company whom we must thank for its enduring success.

Wilson McComb and other MG authorities have covered the early history of the marque in far more detail than would be appropriate here. Nevertheless, it is important to note that among the dedicated group of men Kimber gathered around him were such talented individuals as Sydney Enever, Alec Hounslow and John Thornley, who were destined to spend the rest of their working lives with the company and would play significant parts in the evolution of the postwar sports car and, ultimately, the V8-engined MG.

Into The Postwar Era

The Second World War was followed in Britain by a period of motoring austerity experienced neither before nor since. Not only was petrol severely rationed in the UK, but motoring manufacturers were restricted in the amount of sheet steel they were permitted to acquire. The only way around this obstacle was to increase to an unprecedented

Right: Cecil Kimber, 1888-1945: the genius behind the prewar MG. *(Rover, author collection)*

Below: A youthful Syd Enever stands in the centre of a group of MG Development mechanics at Abingdon in the mid-1930s. *(Rover)*

level the proportion of cars which was exported, thereby gaining extra quotas of sheet steel from the Ministry of Supply. (Everyone remembers or knows the famous 'export or die' maxim.) MG were in the fortunate position of being able to benefit from this situation, having already established a small but intensely loyal following overseas. Even so, they were forced to rationalise their large prewar range to just one model, the TC Midget, which was simply a mildly-improved version of the 1938 TB, hastily produced by the Cowley-based MG design office.

Despite this difficult climate, MG managed to prosper. The American market, accustomed to wallowing in large, comfortable sedans, discovered the 'quaint' little MG sports cars and took to them in a big way; and MG found a similarly warm reception in many other export markets.

Thus the scene was set for rising sales and profits — and the TD Midget of 1949, with its bumpers, disc wheels and a front suspension which would ultimately evolve into the MGB unit, raised sales yet higher. MG could do no wrong, it appeared, and under the wing of the Nuffied Organisation its

Left: Jim O'Neill at work on the design of the MG ZA Magnette in the Cowley drawing office in June 1950. O'Neill already had the body of the TD Midget to his credit and went on to participate in many MG projects including the MGA and MGB. (Jim O'Neill)

future seemed assured, although the picture changed slightly in 1952 when the rival Nuffield and Austin concerns merged to form the British Motor Corporation. This in itself might have had no direct bearing on MG, had it not been for the fact that in charge of Austin was Leonard Lord, a former manager of Morris Motors who had fallen out with Lord Nuffield some years previously. It was Lord who took the helm at BMC and his arrival was followed by a massive programme of rationalisation of engines and transmission units throughout the entire organisation. MG sports cars were of comparatively little importance to Lord, but nevertheless, in John Thornley's words, 'his overall attitude towards us — and to me in particular — has scored above the line'.

An All-New MG Sports Car

Although the TD Midget continued to sell, it was beginning to seem long in the tooth, particularly in the face of more modern opposition from rival companies. What had been good enough in the less-than-innovative immediate postwar years was insufficient to satisfy the higher expectations emerging in the more affluent and adventurous 1950s. At the Cowley-based MG and Riley drawing office, recent ex-Jowett recruit Gerald Palmer came up with a proposal for a new MG sports car which could have been produced in three parallel versions, one with 'traditional' separately styled wings, another with cycle type wings, and the third with a more modern faired-in wing line. However there is little doubt that this proposal, originated outside Abingdon, was viewed by the MG management with little more enthusiasm than they had accorded the various Nuffield proposals for new MGs which had been drafted in the late 1940s.

In 1951 George Philips, who had successfully campaigned a works-prepared TC in the previous two years, was provided by MG with a TD chassis-ed car with sleek aerodynamic lines quite unlike anything ever seen on an MG. Sydney Enever was responsible for this car, registered UMG400, and such was the appeal of its styling that he designed an improved 'road version' using a similar body but with a new chassis, in which the side members were realigned to allow the driver to sit lower in the car. This maroon-coloured car, registered HMO 6 and bearing the prototype number EX175, was finished by the end of the following year and was shown by a proud MG management to their masters at Longbridge — with, as it transpired, monumentally bad timing. Donald Healey, well known for his large and expensive Healey sports cars, had designed a sleek new low-cost sports car, which used the engine from Longbridge's great export hope, the Austin A90 Atlantic, a car in which Leonard Lord took a great deal of interest. Healey exhibited the prototype Healey 100, as it was called, at Earls Court in October 1952, where it was one of the sensations of the show. Leonard Lord saw the car and was

struck immediately by the facts that it used the under-utilised Austin A90 engine and that it had already been developed for production. Never one to prevaricate, Lord promptly agreed to build the car in much larger numbers than Healey had originally envisaged, and thus was launched the Austin-Healey 100. Consequently, when the MG management presented their EX175 prototype, together with a request for capital investment to put the car into production, Lord was less than receptive and told them in no uncertain terms to continue producing the TD. Thus the TD soldiered on, first in Mark II guise and then as the TF, which was little more than a facelift. By this time, however, it was becoming increasingly obvious that the traditional MG Midget had had its day. Despite an inevitable feeling of disappointment in the Abingdon camp, John Thornley was able to develop a special relationship and understanding with Lord which in due course was of benefit to the MG factory: 'Decisions which seemed to go against Abingdon's interests were naturally resented but there was never anything discriminatory or spiteful about them. Most of Leonard Lord's decisions, when viewed with hindsight, are seen to have been well justified. Take as an example the absorbtion of MG by Morris Motors in 1934; he wrote finis to all that we have come to know as Triple-M and all hell broke loose. But, by reverting to the old basis of quantity-produced units, sales took off'.

Similarly, Thornley is surprisingly generous about the decision to build the Austin-Healey in preference to MG's proposal: 'When (Lord) put his foot down on the MGA prototype it was a perfectly rational thing for him to do. He had just bought the Healey 100 and, to his eyes, it and the MGA were clearly aimed at the same market and it didn't make sense to him to have to tool two cars. It wasn't until I had pestered the life out of him, supported strongly by screams from the USA, that he saw the point'.

Eventually, following the poor reception of the TF in North America, the BMC management saw that action was called for if MG sales were to be maintained. As a result, Syd Enever was appointed Chief Engineer at a new design office in the Abingdon factory, with the initial brief of turning EX175 into reality. This he did, developing the car under the prototype number EX182 and aiming for a launch in the summer of 1955.

Thornley, who had been General Manager at MG since 1952, recalls: 'It may be presumptuous of me but I fancy that, in the period between 1952 and the time Lord gave me the go-ahead, some of my enthusiasm rubbed off on him because, from that moment on, all was sweetness and light. From general conversation within BMC I got the impression that I was just about the only senior executive who had not, at one time or another, caught the rough edge of his tongue. We became friends to the point where I was still in touch with him, at a personal and private level, after he retired'.

It was by virtue of this relationship that Thornley had much more influence on Abingdon's affairs than some people have given him credit for: 'I did not have to work on him very hard to get him the see the sense of a BMC Competitions Department'. What soon became known as the 'comps' department was established early in 1955, and Thornley had the inspired idea of promoting the forthcoming car by entering three prototypes at Le Mans. As it transpired, the MGA could not be made ready for launch prior to the June Le Mans race, but the three cars raced as prototypes, this status in itself enhancing both media attention and public interest. By September 1955, the production cars were ready and the MG Series MGA was launched to great public and critical acclaim,

marking a clear break with the traditional 'square rigger' shape which had characterised MG sports cars since Kimber's days.

During what Thornley recalls as the 'critical period' — from 1952 until the clearance for the MGA — there was more at stake than simply the commitment to a new model: 'What was of overriding importance to me was the survival of Abingdon. Had the MGA been denied us, then MG Abingdon would not have continued beyond 1960 at the latest'.

A period of success followed. The MGA evolved through a number of versions, even spawning a more powerful but rather highly-strung twin-cam example. However, events in the motoring world never stand still. Production of MGAs rose to a total of well over 100,000, but as MG found themselves up against increasingly tough opposition from both British and Continental rivals, circumstances again forced them into consideration of a replacement model.

First thoughts on the subject assumed the retention of the Enever-designed MGA chassis, and to that end a number of prototypes were schemed by Jim O'Neill under the experimental code of EX205, including one bodied rather flamboyantly by the Italian coachbuilder Frua. At about this time a young engineer named Don Hayter joined the company from Aston Martin as a senior layout draughtsman. Don had gained experience in the rarefied field of aircraft design, and had exhibited a flair for the design of stressed bodies which would prove useful in the design of the MGA replacement.

It was soon realised that the retention of the MGA chassis was an obstacle to progress, hampering both the development of the lines and the stiffness of any car using it. It was decided instead to develop a monocoque body design. Today monocoque bodies are almost universal, but at the end of the 1950s they were still virtually in their infancy and had never been employed for an open sports car.

Syd Enever, Jim O'Neill and Don Hayter may all be credited for much of the groundwork put into the car which would become the MGB, launched to great acclaim in September 1962. Abingdon found that they had another winner on their hands: output soared, with a three-quarter increase in MG production over the last year in which the MGA was produced, and the car's enthusiastic reception in the USA led to BMC's establishing a new wholly-owned import base at Leonia, New Jersey. Clearly MG's star was in the ascendant.

The Successful 'Sixties

The 1960s were boom years for the British economy, with industries prospering as living standards rose. Unfortunately, though, rapid increases in output were not always matched by sufficient investment in new equipment; there was a tendency in the United Kingdom to avoid major investment in the replacement of essential production equipment, which meant that plant and facilities became outdated and often ill-equipped to deal with multiplying demand.

The British Government *did* offer incentives to manufacturers to invest, but the frequent catch was that they would have to build new facilities in selected development areas rather than invest in their existing ones. Consequently, many large manufacturers were encouraged to invest heavily in new factories in unfamiliar locations (and without a ready local market in experienced labour) whilst their existing factories suffered from under-investment.

The British Motor Corporation was, by the start of the new decade, eight years old but had still not carried through enough rationalisation of its constituent parts, which very often seemed to operate like different outposts of some far-flung Empire. In 1961 the powerful Leonard Lord stood down in favour of George Harriman, who had for many years been Lord's right-hand man and had assumed the post of BMC Managing Director in 1956. Lord and Harriman were firmly wedded to the goal of continuing expansion, and in order to achieve this whilst complying with Government policy they sanctioned the building of new facilities remote from their established production bases at Cowley and Longbridge. In addition, money was invested overseas in new factories: BMC set up in South Africa, Australia, Italy (Innocenti), Spain (Authi) and Belgium (Seneffe).

In 1959 the revolutionary ADO15 Mini was launched, followed during the ensuing five years by the ADO16 1100 and the much larger ADO17 1800. The Mini has justifiably earned its place in history as a fine example of economical transport for four adults; but the little car was not only at the low-priced and hence less profitable end of the market but was also, it transpired, being sold at a price seriously below what its costs should have dictated.

The car which BMC dealers really wanted was a larger and smartly-styled family vehicle, so when the 1100 range was launched in 1962 they welcomed it wholeheartedly. Sales of the 1100 remained solid for many years, representing around a third of the entire UK car market and holding the number one sales spot for a number of years. Its major rival during the period was the Ford Cortina, and it is significant that whereas Ford developed their big seller during the decade (introducing rebodied Mark II and Mark III versions in 1966 and 1970) BMC did nothing of great significance to change ADO16.

If the Mini and the 1100 were successes for BMC, they were offset to some extent by some noteworthy blunders. Two of

*Above: John Thornley (second from left) and Syd Enever (fourth from left) pose proudly alongside the 50,000th sports car built in a single year (1959) at Abingdon. Production of Rileys had been moved to Cowley and the MG ZB Magnette had been discontinued the previous year, so in 1959 Abingdon were building only sports cars.
(Rover, courtesy Haymarket archives)*

the more obvious were the ADO17, which was generally perceived as being too large for its market position, and the ADO61 Austin Three-Litre, which was in reality an unnecessary extravagance, made all the more painfully apparent once the mergers took place in the latter half of the decade.

In 1962, MG had much to be proud of. Successes with the record-breaking cars in the previous decade, and the growing popularity of their sports cars in export markets, meant that the MG name was a beacon of national pride. The marque was truly the jewel in the BMC crown. The MGB story is described in the following chapter, but it is appropriate here to consider the marque in its wider context. In 1961 a badge-engineered version of the Austin-Healey Sprite appeared as the MG Midget, reviving the popular model name which had lapsed with the discontinuation of the TF in 1955 (the new Midget was at one stage destined to be christened the MGD). At the autumn 1962 Motor Show, BMC unveiled alongside the 'B an MG version of the ADO16 1100 saloon, which was available in an export-only two-door version, aimed primarily at the North American market, where it was hoped to cash in on the MG name (there is evidence to show that this car was almost the MGC 1100!). At the top of the MG range was the Farina-styled Magnette MkIII, whose narrow track and poor performance were partially addressed in the MkIV version which appeared late in 1961.

The MG family, therefore, comprised two Abingdon-built sports cars and two Cowley-built saloons — the widest variety of MGs which had been on offer at any one time since before the war. The management at MG had every reason to feel cautiously optimistic, even if they sometimes wondered about the wisdom of their superiors. However, MG's fortunes were inseparably linked to those of their parent company and there were many problems outside Abingdon's sphere of influence which were to have grave consequences.

Leyland: The Wilderness Years

UK car production in the 1960s was largely dominated by the rival ambitions of three companies — the giant British Motor Corporation, the US-owned Ford Motor Co. and the much smaller but more aggressive Leyland organisation, run by a management drawn chiefly from its Triumph subsidiary. In 1966, Sir William Lyons responded to overtures from George Harriman, and Jaguar (with its Daimler and Coventry Climax subsidiaries) merged with BMC to form British Motor Holdings, or BMH for short. BMC had also been attempting to woo the successful Rover company, which had only recently acquired the rights to the Buick V8 engine (in 1964), since Rover had become vulnerable following BMC's acquisition of the independent Pressed Steel Company (which supplied Rover bodies) in 1965. In the event, however, BMC's Leyland rivals were able to reach an agreement with Rover instead.

The merger between BMC and Jaguar had no immediate bearing upon MG, since Jaguar were in no real sense competitors, though the union seemed, on the face of it, to offer a number of possible benefits to the Abingdon concern. Various BMC divisions, including MG, were encouraged to look into the Jaguar cupboard, as a result of which a number of ideas were investigated including various possible schemes for replacing the Austin-Healey 3000 and for the imminent MGC. And it is interesting to consider the thoughts which took place in BMC about a larger 'Austin Morris' sports car which, had it come to fruition, would undoubtedly have had some effect on MG.

In his book *Austin Healey: The Story of the Big Healeys*, Geoff Healey relates how he and his father were struck dumb by a Longbridge-originated project to build a 'super sports car' to replace the Austin-Healey 3000. This car, coded variously ADO30, S4 or XC512, and presumably intended to sit above the MGC in the corporate sports car line-up, used Hydrolastic suspension, all-new bodywork and the Rolls-Royce four-litre engine. Known irreverently as 'Fireball XL5' (after a contemporary Gerry Anderson TV series), the project consumed vast amounts of money and resources before it was abandoned. Its abandonment was the result of pressure from Sir William Lyons, who would not sanction a later version with his twin-cam XK engine in place of the Rolls-Royce unit, since he clearly saw it as a potential competitor to the Jaguar E-Type. Sir William remained a powerful influence throughout the mergers and various other projects from other divisions would be aborted in the following years due to his intervention.

The Healeys, meanwhile, investigated their own scheme for a four-litre Rolls-Royce-engined version of the 'Big Healey', which would have used a Jaguar gearbox and would have been built at Abingdon if it had reached production. This project, carried out in consultation with Syd Enever, was given the BMC code number of ADO24. Only two prototypes were built before the project was cancelled in 1968, due to general financial constraints and specific doubts about the cost and viability of making the car meet US legal requirements (which had been one of the main reasons for the discontinuation of the Big Healey itself); it was also overtaken by events which would affect the future of all the marques within the company.

Rather as there had been overtures between the Austin and Nuffield organisations in the late 'forties and early 'fifties, preliminary discussions took place between BMC (and, subsequently, BMH) and their opposite numbers at Leyland well in advance of the merger which took place in 1968. At that stage, thoughts were of a merger of equals; only when negotiations were within sight of completion did the problems of the mammoth BMC organisation truly emerge. The complete picture showed that whilst there were a number of successful products on sale, there appeared to have been insufficient thought given to the future, and this would have dire consequences for the new British Leyland organisation which came into being.

Leyland's origins dwelt in the last years of the nineteenth century. Throughout the inter-war years the company's buses and lorries earned it a formidable reputation; by the late 1950s, its finances were buoyant, and by the turn of the decade it had begun searching for ways to expand its range of operations. In 1961, Leyland acquired the Standard-Triumph company. A year later, Donald Stokes, Leyland's highly successful Export Director, became Managing Director, and the year after that the Leyland Motor Corporation was formed, having acquired in AEC its major rival.

As we have seen, despite the logic of a tie-up between Rover and BMC, the Solihull company became part of the Leyland Organisation in the spring of 1967, not long after the BMC/Jaguar deal had been struck. By then, at the promptings of the Labour government, exploratory discussions were being held between Leyland and BMH about the possibility of a merger. The need for this merger, at least from BMC's viewpoint, soon became more apparent; as Jonathan Wood states in his motor industry history *Wheels of Misfortune*, by the end of 1968 the writing was on the wall. 'In November BMH announced that it had made a pre-tax loss of £3.2 million. Leyland, by contrast, had made an £18 million profit.'

✧

At Triumph, one of the masterminds of the company's products in the 1960s had been an engineer named Harry Webster, whose list of credits included the Triumph Herald, the front-wheel-drive 1300 and the V8 engine which was developed specifically for the Stag. Webster's record made him an understandable choice for the post of Engineering Director at the former Austin headquarters at Longbridge. Not surprisingly, he was soon surrounded by new or ex-Triumph management as the old BMC guard faded away.

By August 1968, Webster had put forward a plan which called for the end of badge engineering (and hence cars like the MG Magnette and the entire Riley range) and a distinct marque policy for the Austin and Morris ranges. The Austins would have advanced engineering (front-wheel drive) but more conservative styling, whilst the Morrises would place greater emphasis on style but would be conventionally engineered. It was an idea that was never fully pursued, and today Harry Webster bemoans the fact that the amount of money spent by British Leyland on engineering was only half of what it should have been. Even so, the basis of this policy led in due course to the Allegro (1973) and Marina (1971), although the 'last BMC car', the Maxi, was launched first.

Meanwhile at the Rover and Triumph divisions of the combine, there were other difficulties in rationalising two problematically overlapping ranges; both divisions had plans to replace their two-litre saloon ranges, but obviously there was little to be gained by producing two competing ranges within the same company. As a result, though not without some procrastination, the Triumph and Rover concerns were merged first into 'Rover-Triumph' and later the 'Specialist Cars Division' (from which MG, with their ties to the Austin Morris framework, were significantly excluded until 1977). Rover and Triumph plans were eventually rationalised: Rover were put in charge of producing the large executive saloon replacement for the Triumph 2000 and Rover P6 ranges, whilst Triumph assumed responsibility for the engines, other than the famous Rover V8. This project eventually resulted in the Rover SD1 hatchback.

As compensation for losing their flagship, Triumph were allowed to design most of the replacement for their mid-range saloon (soon to reach its ultimate evolution as the Dolomite) in the form of the 'SD2', and to consider the replacement of their TR6, Spitfire and GT6 sports cars, which fell under the 'Bullet' code name.

All of this meant that MG felt increasingly isolated and remote from senior management. Even though the Abingdon plant was undeniably the corporate sports car facility and as such had no significant internal competition, the effective takeover of their Austin-Morris masters by people who had come from Triumph, their deadly sports car rivals, filled MG staff with trepidation. It was no coincidence that a number of the better-known MG faces slipped quietly away during the next few years.

Plans were drawn up for an MG sports coupé, coded ADO68, which would have been related to the Morris Marina, but this project was cancelled around 1970. As seen in photographs, it would undoubtedly have been a stunning contender in the sports coupé market (though it would probably have been built at Cowley rather than Abingdon). Also considered but shelved was a targa-top coupé prototype styled at Longbridge by Rob Owen and built to his design by Michelotti, based on the Mini 1275GT floorpan and coded ADO70.

MG themselves looked at two specific projects as possible replacements for the MGB. The first, codenamed EX234, was styled by Pininfarina and bore a resemblance to Alfa Romeo's pretty Duetto Spyder of 1966. It was envisaged that this car would be produced in both 1.3- and 1.8-litre versions, thereby replacing both the MG Midget and the MGB, and it was designed to utilise the Hydrolastic suspension system. Unfortunately the project was overtaken by events in the parent company, together with the need for Abingdon to concentrate on the problems posed by increasing US legislation, and EX234

Above: *The first significant effect of the Leyland merger on the MG range was the introduction in September 1969 of the controversial recessed matt black grille, the fitting of distinctive Rostyle wheels and of small BL badges on both front wings. (Autocar)*

Below: *What might have been… this Aston Martin proposal for a 1981 MGB roadster incorporated a number of ideas which had been put forward by BL themselves, including the restyled front bumper. Restyling was by the late William Towns, and it was intended that a rebodied MGB would have followed for 1983. (Roger Stowers)*

was mothballed. Abingdon's other proposal was the mid-engined ADO21, which emerged in 1970 and would have utilised a choice of the Austin Maxi E series 1748cc straight four or the E6 2227 engine. The chassis of ADO21 featured sophisticated De Dion rear suspension, the brain child of MG Chief Chassis Engineer Terry Mitchell; most striking, though, was the Harris Mann styling, which featured a very advanced sharp-nosed wedge shape and would undoubtedly have marked as remarkable a break with the MGB as the MGA had with the TF Midget.

Sadly, the MG project had to compete with the rival Triumph Bullet proposal and, following a fact finding mission to the USA by Triumph engineers, a corporate decision was made to pursue a conventional rear-wheel-drive sports car (using the Triumph running gear) with advanced styling (inspired by ADO21). It was also planned at an early stage that the new car would be badged as both MG and Triumph versions, although the role of the Abingdon plant in all this remained unclear.

Against this background, the old guard at MG were understandably pessimistic. They had, after all, seen two of their best contenders for replacements for their principal product abandoned, and they were increasingly inundated with vehicle emissions and impact resistance requirements, whilst investment in their core business was sadly lacking. The opportunity to produce a V8-engined version of the MGB can be seen in

that context as a potential lifeline for the Abingdon plant. It was greeted with great enthusiasm and no little relief.

New Directions

The over-riding spectacle of the Leyland years was that of one of the world's major motor manufacturers sliding inexorably into decline, towards the automotive equivalent of a third world power. A constant succession of strikes and internal conflicts within the company combined with dramatic changes in external market forces to drive the company to 'cut off its limbs to survive'. The Triumph TR7, in which millions of pounds were invested, was dogged from the outset by poor quality control and industrial strife and failed dismally to live up to expectations. (Some writers have commented retrospectively that the TR7 was given an undeservedly bad press, but the author well remembers examining his cousin's brand new Speke-built TR7 in 1977 and listing over a hundred quite unacceptable faults!)

Plans for the production of a 16-valve version of the TR7 (which would have been the TR7 Sprint) and the long-wheelbase Lynx were both shelved, and thoughts of an MG-badged version of the TR7 were suspended, though this project was briefly reconsidered a few years later, after the closure of the Abingdon factory.

During this period a new Chairman, in the shape of Michael Edwardes, was appointed, following an embarrassingly long period when no one seemed to want the job. Edwardes decided to seize the bull by the horns and try to tackle the task of rationalising the constituent parts of the BL empire, a job which many commentators were saying should have been done long before. In 1979, the arrival of a new Conservative Government, with its commitment to de-nationalisation and its belief that industry should run itself with minimal or no Government intervention, was greeted happily by the financial community and led to a dramatic upturn in the value of sterling. However, while this was good news for the country's cash reserves, it was a bitter pill for British exporters to swallow — none more so than BL, whose sports car output was based almost entirely on the expectation of sustained high demand in North America. Given this turn of events, and the ever-increasing American demands for safety and environmental controls, it is hardly surprising that the demise of the MG factory and its products became a common subject of discussion, a matter not of 'if' but 'when'.

The closure of the Abingdon factory and the demise of the MG sports car were soon succeeded by the end of the TR7 and the V8-engined TR8 — the latter a car which should have taken over the mantle of the MGB GT V8. By the end of 1981, British Leyland volume-production sports cars were no more. An attempt was made to re-enter the North American saloon car market with the Rover SD1 but, after enormous sums had been spent on making the V8 engine comply with US emissions legislation, it was wholly unsuccessful.

Yet the early 1980s also saw the beginnings of a renaissance for the drastically slimmed-down company. A change of name for the volume car division to 'Austin Rover' coincided with the launch of the Austin Metro, a competent and well designed car which almost certainly saved the company from oblivion. In view of the widespread dismay caused by the closure of the MG factory, it was perhaps no surprise that the famous badge soon reappeared on the nose of a high-performance version

Abingdon's Last Days

The fate of the Abingdon factory was for a long time a subject of widespread conjecture and debate. In its earlier days, the factory had manufactured a large proportion of its output in-house, but after the war it increasingly became what John Thornley called an 'assembly shop', building cars from components supplied by other factories. A visitor to MG's premises during its last years might well have witnessed transporters loaded with what appeared to be almost complete cars *entering* the factory. Bodyshell assembly, painting and even most of the trimming were carried out at Leyland's Swindon plant, before Abingdon could start work on them, while engines, gearboxes and other components were also shipped in from elsewhere. This arrangement was hardly unique to MG, but it did contribute strongly to the situation wherein Abingdon's fate was linked inextricably to factors outside its control.

As early as 1976, there were articles published in the *Abingdon Herald* suggesting that BL were planning to close the factory and sell the buildings. Even though the rumours proved unfounded, they did nothing to alleviate the uncertainty already being experienced by MG's strongly-committed workforce.

In 1978 MG were finally drawn into the BL 'Specialist Cars' fold, joining the division known as 'Jaguar Rover Triumph' (JRT), and for a while it seemed that their future might after all be secure. Publicly, BL management personnel were at pains to state that they recognised the value of the marque and that they had no plans which would damage or eliminate it. Behind the scenes, work was proceeding on the O-Series engine transplant, with the promise of dramatically improved performance for the 1980 model year MGB. The O-series unit had been designed from the outset with the MGB in mind, but with the shift in exchange rates brought about by the election of Margaret Thatcher's government in 1979, exports were hard hit and the MG, with its crucial reliance on the North American market, was one of the foremost casualties. Coupled with this turn of events was the sweeping programme of rationalisation within the BL organisation, initiated by Michael Edwardes, so that by the late summer Abingdon's situation was more critical than it had ever been.

The announcement of the end of MG manufacture at Abingdon came in September 1979. During the previous week, ironically enough, there had been a jamboree in the town to celebrate 50 years of production there and people had been raising their glasses to the prospect of many more years to come. Included in BL's announcement was the statement that, even though the MGB would be discontinued, the factory would still have a role to play. Among the ventures planned for it were work on the recently-announced Honda 'Bounty' joint project, the preparation of special-specification vehicles and an involvement in competition activities.

For a time, an offer from Alan Curtis of Aston Martin seemed to offer some hope for the MGB and for the factory continuing to build complete MG cars. Plans were drawn up for a revised MGB for 1981, the styling of which drew upon existing Leyland proposals, but ultimately the finance could not be found and the bid collapsed. By this time, too, BL had abandoned their plans for the factory and in October 1980, after 51 years during which well over a million cars had been built, MG's gates were closed for the last time.

For a while, though perhaps more in hope than expectation, there was talk of 'Broadside', which was basically an MG-badged version of the TR7, expected to utilise the O-Series engine. But it was not to be; within a year of Abingdon's closure, the TR7 and TR8 had followed both the MGB and the factory into the history books.

---

of the Metro, accompanied by a remarkable number of MG logos distributed all over the car in a manner akin to the days of Cecil Kimber some 60 years beforehand. So successful was the MG Metro — particularly in export markets — that the idea was repeated for the next new models of the 1980s, the Maestro and Montego. The company tried gamely to play up the fact that there had been many MG saloons in the marque's earlier history, but the public was never really convinced; even though sales were healthy, the association of the MG badge with sports cars was so much stronger that media rumours of a new MG sporting model soon became commonplace.

✧

In 1986 Austin Rover returned to North America, selling the new Austin Rover/Honda joint project Rover 800 as the 'Sterling'. Despite early promise and favourable test reports, the project failed to live up to all that had been hoped for from it and within four years the company was left licking its wounds. The launch of the Sterling had led to yet more conjecture about the possibility of a new MG sports car which could have been marketed alongside it, but unfortunately the company had many more pressing uses for its money, and although a number of design studies were carried out, they came to nothing.

Below: The Range Rover: a timeless classic like the MGB and the Rover V8 engine itself, its success helped make the MG RV8 possible. (Rover)

Left: John Thornley pictured outside his former home in Abingdon with his faithful MGB GT, 'MG 1'.

If the Sterling episode is a source of regret for what might have been, the story of the successful launch of the Range Rover was an object lesson in how to open up a hitherto unrecognised market niche. Much work had been done towards the end of the 'seventies in developing the V8 engine for fuel injection and catalytic converters, so the ground work for the Range Rover's introduction was already well advanced. The remarkable success of the prestigious 4x4 undeniably helped to ensure that the V8 engine remained part of the Rover stable, even after its use in the mainstream car range was discontinued with the last of the Rover SD1 range.

In 1985 'Range Rover of North America' was established, and in 1987 the Range Rover was launched in the USA. Before long, people were queuing to buy the car, placing deposits well in advance of delivery. Range Rovers soon became an essential accessory for the rich and famous, with such people as actor Jack Nicholson and singer/actress Cher among their owners. The enormous success of the Range Rover led in 1993 to the USA re-launch of the Land Rover (absent from North America since 1974) and the planned launch of the Land Rover Discovery in 1994, all of them powered by the classic V8 engine.

In March 1988 the Rover Group was finally returned to the private sector and was acquired by British Aerospace. Parallel with this came a rationalisation of the two principal marques, with the Austin name fading from the picture in favour of the more up-market Rover brand, the process being termed 'Roverisation'. The MG versions of the Metro, Maestro and Montego were discontinued, and for a while it looked to many outside the company as if the MG badge would follow the Austin badge into oblivion. In fact, there had been yet another revolution in the corridors of Canley, Longbridge and Cowley, and with it had come the final abandonment of so-called 'badge

engineering', a legacy of the BMC of 30 years before which had become outmoded and unpopular.

Rover management made it clear that there would be no MG-badged derivatives of the mainstream Rover range; any MG products which appeared would be more in keeping with the marque's sports car heritage, whilst using appropriate hardware from the corporate cupboard. Thus there would be no MG versions of the Rover 200, 400, 600 or 800 ranges; future MGs would have unique bodies and would be clearly identifiable as MGs without observers needing to check the badge. Against the backdrop of this promising sea-change, the stage was set for the re-launch of the Octagon on a special limited-production car which would, perhaps, pave the way for a higher-volume sports car. The story of how that re-launch was conceived and achieved, and of the motoring world's reaction, is told further on.

By the beginning of 1994, the five-year period during which British Aerospace had been required to retain control of the Rover Group had elapsed. Speculations about the possibility of a merger, an increased shareholding by Honda or a takeover by another company were ended suddenly at the end of January, when it was announced that BAe would be selling their 80 percent stake in the Rover Group to the German giant, BMW. In the course of his statement at the time of the takeover, BMW Chairman Bernd Pischetsrieder (the nephew, incidentally, of Sir Alec Issigonis) observed that '...we wish to preserve our mutual heritage from which very specific brand and product features have developed over the decades... Obviously we are looking forward in particular to the temptation — and opportunity — to reinstate in the coming years some of the great British automobile marques so renowned in the past.'

MG enthusiasts can read into that what they will.

2

The MGB, The MGC & The Rover V8 Engine

Evolution Of The MGB

No sooner was the MGA in production than the design staff at Abingdon were giving serious consideration to the nature of its successor. As early as November 1955 — barely months after the MGA's launch — John Thornley and Syd Enever produced a joint paper, 'Suggested Design and Development Programme for Abingdon Products,' which argued strongly that all future cars built at Abingdon should have separate chassis frames. Even so, Thornley recalls, by the middle of the following year MG were scratching around with the beginnings of what would become the MGB, which of course ended up with a monocoque body!

In 1957, production of the Austin-Healey 100/6, which had evolved from the Healey 100, was transferred from Longbridge to Abingdon, along with design responsibility for it. This meant that the MG design office became concerned not only with a replacement for the MGA but also with the eventual need to replace the Big Healey as well. The need to rationalise expenditure at Abingdon, problems with Jensen (who built the Austin-Healey bodies on a sub-contract basis) and the likelihood that BMC would be unlikely to sanction two

totally unrelated new MG sports cars in the medium and upper sector of the market made it inevitable that a common successor for both cars would be considered, with the possibility of both Austin-Healey- and MG-badged versions being produced.

John Thornley points out that this dual requirement partly accounted for the large gap which eventually appeared between the back of the radiator and the front of the engine in the MGB, making it some six inches longer than it strictly needed to be and contributing strongly to its impeccable handling.

Jim O'Neill, then in charge of body design at Abingdon, remembers well the beginnings of the design of the MGA replacement: 'The lines of the MGB were the result of a visit I made with Syd Enever to the Geneva Motor Show. Sydney's designs were invariably started on the backs of cigarette packets — or anything else that happened to be lying around — and this time was no exception. Sydney wanted the headlamps to be set in scollops in the wings, and in the flattish area between the headlamps an elongated traditional MG radiator grille. On our return to Abingdon I drew up a $1/4$-scale drawing and had a wooden model made up in the Morris

Right: Launched at the 1962 Earls Court Motor Show, the MGB is seen here next to the Magnette (with a perspex bootlid to demonstrate its luggage capacity) and the MG 1100 which was also making its debut. (Autocar)

Top: Chief Body Engineer Jim O'Neill receiving the IBCAM coachwork award for the MGB from Lord Camden at the Royal Automobile Club in 1962. (Jim O'Neill)

Above: There was a great deal of controversy shortly after the launch of the MGB about its resemblance to Renault's Floride convertible. Former MG staff are understandably reluctant to admit it, but the author has been shown evidence by one of them which shows that the argument contained more than a grain of truth. But it would be unfair to suggest that the Floride served as anything more than inspiration or that the resemblance was more than superficial. (Haymarket Archives)

Below: The engine bay of a later chrome-bumper MGB. The large gap forward of the radiator was a deliberate means of ensuring space for a bigger engine. (Autocar)

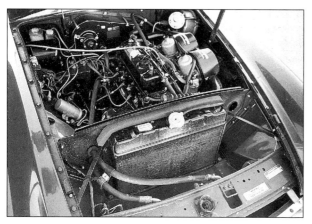

Motors Experimental Shop. This had a very rounded body side section, much like the E-Type Jaguar, but the wheelbase was much too short. It looked more like a dumpy little pig than a sports car — in fact I called it 'the pig'. However, with the body sides flattened, it virtually turned into the MGB we know today. I remember using Austin A40 tail-lamps and a Ford bumper section which they agreed we could use provided we paid half the tooling cost.'

The development of EX205 — described in the EX register as 'MG 2-seater (ADO23)' — began in the summer of 1957. Jim O'Neill: 'Because we'd had the Austin-Healey dropped in our laps, my assistant Denis Williams was overstretched and we needed another draughtsman. That was when Don Hayter joined us.'

The idea of retaining a separate chassis was soon abandoned (although the Frua-bodied MGA was drawn up as EX205/2) and a new project code, EX214, was allocated to the MGA replacement in June 1958. Don Hayter then began to refine and develop the basic shape schemed by O'Neill and Enever. The following year, EX214 was superseded by the formal BMC ADO23 project code. The styling evolved gradually into the familiar blunt-nosed broad-grille MGB shape, starting from a shape with clear overtones of MGA nose and Frua MGA-inspired tail. Don Hayter states that the pronounced rounded 'tumble-home' of the sills was a deliberate ploy to ensure that the body of the MGB would appear longer, lower and hence sleeker than it really was. Thus the low body style theme associated with the MGA was retained even though the MGB featured much taller, more substantial doors than its predecessor. (It is interesting to note how this effect has been deliberately changed on the new RV8, whose sills have been flared outwards in an effort to 'beef up' the body shape.)

Quite early on, it was felt that the new car should employ independent rear suspension, a feature becoming much more common on Italian and German rivals and achieving significant improvements in handling and ride quality. There was also, no doubt, an enthusiasm among some of the longer-serving members of MG's staff to see an 'IRS' MG sports car in the range; the only previous instance had been the shortlived R-type single-seater of 1935, which had been killed off with the abandonment of factory racing.

The major obstacle to putting the new car into production was the cost of body tooling, an expense which would subsequently lead John Thornley to doubt whether another sports car would ever be sanctioned by his masters at Longbridge. Thornley, however, was able to pull off a master stroke by persuading the Pressed Steel body plant to accept an initial cost slashed by more than half in return for enhanced royalties on each body built — an arrangement which ensured that the complex unitary MGB bodyshell was tooled up to Abingdon's requirements and which was of benefit to both MG and Pressed Steel throughout the MGB's production life.

With these terms agreed, work began on producing the body tools in early 1960. Meanwhile, MG continued the necessary development work on the running gear for the new car, and in the process some fundamental changes of heart took place. The first problems concerned the engine, for although MG had designed the MGB from the outset in the expectation that it would most probably be introduced with the trusty B-Series four cylinder in-line engine, the Longbridge engineers had been working on a proposed family of V4 and V6 units, which were intended to replace and rationalise the entire mid and large BMC engine ranges. As Roy Brocklehurst

Above: The elegant Pininfarina-refined lines of the MGB GT first appeared at the 1965 Show. (Autocar)

remembered many years later: 'We were often used by Longbridge as a sort of experimental department — we fitted the V4 engine in an MGA (EX216) and subsequently tried it in the first MGB; later we were involved with oil temperature problems on the ADO17 (1800 saloon) which were eventually solved by reducing the oil levels'.

It soon became apparent, however, that the V4 engines in particular were not particularly refined, and the considerable cost of developing and productionising the new engines, coupled with their poorer packaging efficiency in the increasingly important transverse front-wheel-drive Austin/Morris applications, eventually led the BMC hierarchy to abandon the project entirely. This decision, coupled with the discontinuation of the MGA twin-cam engine, left MG in something of a quandary — although a contemporary of Syd Enever recalls that Enever did not like the uneven exhaust beat of the V4 unit. The MGB was clearly going to be somewhat heavier than the MGA, and increasingly higher performance sports car yardsticks clearly meant that something would have to be done to prevent the embarrassing prospect of an MGB slower than its predecessor. (On test when powered by the 1622cc B-Series engine, the car struggled into the mid-nineties, whilst the same engine in the MGA achieved a top speed of over 100mph.)

Ultimately, MG found their choice restricted by the availability of power units which would be shared with other BMC mainstream vehicles. One possibility had been a four-cylinder derivative of the big Austin C-Series (fitted to the Austin Westminster and Austin Healey 3000) but although considered by MG, this engine was never more than a half-serious proposal and therefore unlikely to find a home in the MGB.

The twin-cam engine had earned itself a reputation as being too highly strung for regular road use and had been discontinued whilst the MGA was still in full production.

The V4 engine (Abingdon never experimented with any V6 versions, according to Roy Brocklehurst) was, as we have seen, ultimately stillborn, so Abingdon were back with the trusty B-Series! One more fortunate aspect of the abandonment of the V4 engine was the fact that the large Issigonis-designed ADO17 (known subsequently as the 'land crab') had originally been intended to use this new unit; BMC's change of heart meant that the B-Series would have to be used instead and be enlarged still further to provide the necessary power for the new large car. The B-Series was given its final stretch to 1798cc and, although ADO17 was not scheduled for introduction until 1964, the MGB was able to benefit from the larger engine capacity in advance. As Roy Brocklehurst's point about experimentation suggests, doubtless BMC were happy to let MG sort out any teething problems with the larger unit before the bigger and heavier saloons came along. (The ADO17 engine benefited from five main bearings as opposed to the three of all previous B-series units, a refinement extended to the MGB in 1964.)

The second major rethink concerned the rear suspension for, as already described, MG had been determined to provide their new sports car with the sophistication of an independent rear end. By the middle of 1960, while Pressed Steel were already preparing tooling drawings, the first recognisable MGB prototype (initially based on drawing EX214/12 but soon formalised under the BMC ADO23 code, as drawing ADO23/163) was built with a coil-sprung rear axle, although MGA 'mules' had been run for some time with IRS. When Don Hayter came to draw up ADO23/163, there was no suitable 'independent' differential unit available, which was the reason why this version used a live rear axle located on trailing arms with coil springs and a transverse Panhard rod.

Above: ERX 498C was one of the earliest GTs, registered in June 1965, and featured in many contemporary BMC publicity photographs. (Rover)

Problems were soon being encountered during road testing, as seasoned MG testers like Tommy Haig commented bluntly on the car's wayward handling — reporting precisely the opposite, in fact, of what had been hoped for. As Don Hayter put it: 'It was the steering effect caused by the radius of action of the Panhard rod which Tom Haig didn't like.' Various thoughts were given to providing a more sophisticated location for the rear suspension arms, but unfortunately the most potentially successful would also have been the most expensive and was thus ruled out. At the eleventh hour, therefore, Syd Enever decided to revert to a live axle with MGA-style inclined cart springs, necessitating a slight lengthening of the body in the process. By now it was midsummer 1960, but the changes were made in time for Pressed Steel to accommodate them.

By the end of 1961, the specification of the MGB had been more or less finalised, and the first production cars were assembled in May 1962, with an intended launch at the autumn Earls Court Motor Show. BMC's characteristically stylish MG display at Earls Court included a cutaway MGB together with a complete car, alongside the new MG 1100 and the one year-old MG Midget.

The MGB GT

John Thornley was determined that there should be a coupé version of the MGB. As he explained in a letter to the author: 'In the early 'fifties, when we were playing with George Philip's TDs — which finally grew into the MGA — I saw, in a production car race at Silverstone, three DB2/4 Aston Martins running in line ahead and I became obsessed with the thought that they were of the shape which we should pursue. By then the MGA was too far down the road and, mainly

because of the boot-lid, the MGA coupé bore scant relationship to the DB2/4! But when we came to work on the MGB it was a different story. We designed the 'roadster' with the fore-knowledge that it would ultimately have an unstressed top on it but priority was given to the open car as this was the one which would keep the American market open. But when we began to put a top on, it wouldn't go right. After several attempts we sent the car to Pininfarina in Italy and what came back received instant and universal approval. All along we had been trying to retain the roadster windscreen. Pininfarina threw it out, picked up the top rail by a couple of inches, sharpened the corners, and there we were!'

Further help towards finding an answer to the problem of an MGB coupé came from Jim O'Neill, who had been able to draw inspiration from the hardtop supplied as part of the Frua-bodied MGA exercise and whose efforts bore some likeness to the contemporary Aston Martin DB4.

The production version of the MGB GT — known in MG's EX Register as EX227, but still under the ADO23 Austin Morris code shared with the open MGB — was launched to great acclaim in 1965. Its beautiful styling earned it the title of 'the poor man's Aston Martin', a description which happily echoed John Thornley's original inspiration for the car. The high roof of the GT gave the false impression that there was sufficient rear space to accommodate two passengers: the marketing men described the car as a 2+2 which, as anyone who has sat in the back of an MGB GT will testify, was something of an exaggeration.

At the time of its launch, the MGB GT was almost unique in offering a wide opening rear tailgate. This made it an attractively versatile car, equally practical for touring, racing or shopping. Unfortunately, by the time real opposition began to emerge, the two-seat status of the GT put it at something of a disadvantage; it is certain that some European sales were lost in later years to the Ford Capri because of this. Even so, the MGB GT was undeniably a highly seductive package and soon found its own niche in the sports car market.

The MGC

As already noted, the idea for an MGB-based successor to the Big Healey first surfaced in 1957, when responsibility for the six-cylinder Austin-Healey moved from Longbridge to Abingdon. MG always worked well with the Healeys, in an atmosphere of mutual respect, but the success of Donald Healey in persuading Leonard Lord to build his Healey 100 in preference to MG's proposed replacement for the T-Type Midget must surely have rankled at Abingdon. It would hardly have been surprising if some of the Abingdon staff had found an element of poetic justice in their being made principally responsible for a replacement for the Big Healey. Whatever their feelings, parallel with the replacement for the MGA consideration was also being given to a closely-related successor to the Austin-Healey 100/6 (later to become the 3000). An obvious candidate would have been an MGB with the Longbridge-designed V6 engine but of course this engine was never even tried out by Abingdon.

The next option which was seriously considered was an engine which had been developed for the Australian BMC subsidiary and was used with some success in the locally assembled Austin Freeway and Wolseley 24/80. This unit was known as the 24Y Blue Streak Six and had a capacity of 2433cc. It was effectively little more than a six cylinder version of the B-Series, sharing its bore and stroke dimensions with the 1622 four-cylinder unit, and in standard tune it produced around 80bhp at 4350rpm, although this would of course have been expected to have risen in any MG version. Early efforts at tuning the unit — giving around 115bhp at 5200rpm — led to the conclusion that the performance would not have represented a significant enough advance over the MGB, and in any case the Antipodean origins of the unit would have made it an uneconomical proposition. (Even so, as Geoffrey Healey relates in his book *Austin-Healey — The Story of the Big Healeys*, the Australian unit did have the significant advantage of being around 106lbs lighter than the current 2912cc Big Healey C-series unit.)

By this stage, the Healeys were participating in discussions with John Thornley and George Harriman about the possibility of a joint MG/Austin-Healey successor to the 3000, and the parallel projects were designated ADO51/52, with ADO51 being the Austin-Healey and ADO52 the MG.

Particularly attractive to the Healeys was the proposal of a development of the 2660cc four-cylinder engine which had seen service in the Austin A90 and the Austin-Healey 100/4 and was still in limited use in the four-wheel-drive Austin Gypsy and the Austin Taxi. Bearing in mind the considerable competition experience the Healeys had built up with this unit, it is hardly surprising that they were confident it would make a sound basis for a joint MG/Austin-Healey sports car. A good deal of work went into the difficult task of making the engine fit into the MGB (which would have necessitated bonnet bulges not unlike those on the MGC as eventually produced). Ultimately, however, the 2.7-litre four (reduced to 2.5 litres for the project) was abandoned on the grounds that it would have had no application to other vehicles.

Just as the requirement for a larger version of the B-Series for the big ADO17 Austin 1800 saloon had decided the engine choice for the MGB, so the needs of BMC's corporate replacement for the Farina-styled big Austin Westminster and Wolseley 6/110 ultimately settled the question of a power unit for ADO51/52. The new large saloon, codenamed ADO61, would use a refined and re-engineered version of the old

---

The Austin Three-Litre

The Austin Three-Litre (ADO61) was one of the last legacies of BMC to be inherited by the new order at British Leyland in 1968. First thoughts, at the start of the decade, had centred on the use of the same 'Blue Streak' Australian B-series six-cylinder 2433cc unit which was considered for the MGC, but this engine was thought to be insufficiently powerful for the flagship of the Austin line, bearing in mind that it would be replacing the venerable three-litre C-series six.

Following its first appearance in 1967, the Three-Litre promptly disappeared for about twelve months while an improved production version was made ready. As soon as the British Leyland merger had taken place, a number of exercises aimed at improving the car were put in motion. Harry Webster initiated a scheme to replace the heavy cast-iron Austin six-cylinder unit with the 3.5-litre all-alloy Rover V8, and during 1969 personally ran a car thus converted. There were plans for a Wolseley-badged version of ADO61 with this engine and a prototype was apparently built, but the project was abandoned in 1970 — probably because Rover and Triumph were none too happy about the prospect of internal competition from the big 'Austin Morris' car. Nevertheless, a precedent had been set for Austin Morris investigating the use of the V8, leading one to speculate that, if the 'Wolseley 3500' had gone ahead, there might have been an MGC V8 in 1970.

C-series unit, acquiring seven main bearings in lieu of the original's four in the interests of refinement. The Abingdon team had to accept this engine with good grace, but it must have been obvious even at this early stage that it was hardly what they wanted. Quite apart from its massive weight (which the Morris Engines development team had at least promised to reduce), the engine was extremely bulky and would be difficult to fit in the MGB engine bay without significant and expensive structural alterations. Don Hayter recalls that Syd Enever took MG's concerns about the engine to Issigonis: 'Syd tried to get Issigonis to shorten the stroke and both lower the unit by about one-and-a-quarter inches and reduce the weight at the same time. Based on his experience of the old MG engines, he also felt that the exhaust and inlet ports could be modified to improve gas flow, but none of this was accepted.' Abingdon was therefore forced to use the new engine despite its less than ideal specification.

As a result of this, the car which eventually emerged shared little forward of the windscreen with the four-cylinder MGB, other than the wings, bumpers and radiator grille. Even the front suspension unit had to be totally revised, due to the

Above: The MGC was launched in 1967 as the replacement for the legendary Big Healey — a tough act to follow. Production lasted until 1969 and only 8,999 examples were built, approximately half of which were closed GT coupés. (Autocar)

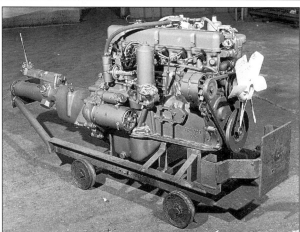

Left: The main problem with the MGC was the weight of the redesigned C-series engine, shown here on a trolley at the MG factory. It was found to be 70lbs heavier than the Abingdon engineers had been led to expect. (Rover)

Below: The MGC was the last MG sports car raced by the factory and might have had a long and successful career had it not been overtaken by events within the parent company. This is the MGC GTS MBL 546E, pictured at Sebring in 1968. (Autocar)

Right: The first appearance of the Rover version of the legendary aluminium V8 engine was in the P5 saloon, at the 1967 Motor Show. Note the distinctive opposed inclined SU carburettor installation, which also appeared in the smaller Rover P6 3500 and subsequently in the majority of Ken Costello's MGB GT V8 conversions. (Autocar)

location of the sump of the big engine, and consequently ADO51/52 was given a unique torsion bar unit.

Understandably, the Healey family had meanwhile been pursuing their own projects, one of which, as we have seen, was with the tacit involvement of MG's Syd Enever. As soon as the ADO51/52 project reached pre-production stage, the Healeys were shown the outcome and they were appalled. The Austin-Healey 3000 MkIV (which came sufficiently close to production that part numbers were assigned and service publications prepared) differed little from the MGC: only a 'Healey' grille (styled by Don Hayter), revised bumper over-riders, an additional sill trim strip and a few other details gave it its own identity.

If this failed to impress Donald and Geoffrey Healey, they were even less enamoured of the new car's engine and its handling, both of which in their opinion left much to be desired. The problem was chiefly that Morris Engines had failed to deliver: the revised C-Series engine was only a little lighter and emphatically more sluggish than the previous version — fine for a three-litre saloon, in other words, which was of course its primary destination. By the time that various ancillaries had been installed, the MGC weighed about 340 lbs more than the contemporary MGB, and most of this lay over the front wheels.

The Healeys decided to play no further part in the project and the Austin-Healey 3000 MkIV was cancelled at a fairly late stage, in 1966. Since it differed so little from the MGC, the costs incurred as a result were minimal, and with BMC increasingly set on 'doing their own thing', the Healey involvement may well have been drawing to a close anyway, even before the Leyland merger led to the end of all external consultancy arrangements.

Whilst the Healeys disliked the MGC, it was recognised by the MG factory too as being far from ideal, but by the time the redesigned engine came along it was probably too late to do much about it. The MGC was launched at the October 1967 Motor Show, where it was proudly displayed on an illuminated turntable. Motoring journalists were less than enthusiastic, expressing their disappointment that a product of the famous Abingdon factory should be so lacking in sporting characteristics. Reports in *Autocar*, *Motor*, *Car* and such influential North American journals as *Road & Track* and *Car & Driver* were all, if not downright critical, depressingly lukewarm.

The 1969 model-year cars were significantly better, but by then the mergers between BMC, Jaguar and Leyland had placed the marque in an entirely different perspective. The MGC was dropped at the end of 1969 (followed two years later by the Austin Three-Litre, which had proved no more successful). The demise of the MGC was regarded with mixed feelings at Abingdon, a natural disappointment being tinged with a certain relief to see the back of it!

John Thornley puts the story into perspective: 'There were two things wrong with the MGC. Firstly it was nose heavy. We all knew that our ideals had gone out of the window the moment we received — and weighed — the first engine. Secondly, motoring correspondents who look objectively at the car they are testing are very thin on the ground. Everybody who had had experience of the MGB tried to chuck the MGC around in a similar manner — and came unstuck. Anyone going to the MGC for the first time — or those who took a completely detached look at it — found it to be a very good, long-legged car in the true grand touring tradition.'

Origins Of The V8 Engine

The 1950s were boom years in the United States, yet the need for European economies to earn dollars meant that an increasing number of British and Continental cars were finding their way across the Atlantic. Volkswagen and other marques began making serious inroads into the US market, generating a demand for a newer, lighter car and opening up a new market sector. American car manufacturers recognised the potential in this sector and, towards the end of the decade, the 'Big Three' — General Motors, Chrysler and Ford — began making serious efforts to develop lighter and more efficient vehicles at the bottom ends of their ranges.

General Motors had been experimenting for some time with aluminium as the basis for engine blocks, some of the results of which appeared in the famous GM show cars of the early 'fifties. It was only natural, therefore, that the Buick Division of General Motors should pursue the design of a production engine using aluminium alloy for its major components. The Buick engine which emerged in 1961, followed a year later by a basically similar but non-interchangeable Oldsmobile version, had a capacity of 215 cubic inches (3531cc) and was largely diecast, a necessity of the high volumes anticipated by GM and one of the features which distinguishes the Buick engine from its Rover offspring.

To solve the problem of wear in the cylinders, it was decided that the most economical approach would be to use integrally cast iron liners; and the aluminium alloy cylinder heads had separate valve seats, a feature which has persisted to this day and the hardness of which is one of the reasons why the V8 engine has proved suitable for unleaded petrol. As had become normal practice for American V8s, hydraulic tappets were used; these require minimal maintenance but have only in recent years become more widely seen in European engines. According to David Wall, who was involved with the Rover version of the engine from the beginning until his retirement early in 1993, the metallurgy between the camshaft and the lifter is critical; to this day, Rover engines use hydraulic tappets sourced in the USA (from GM) and the camshaft casting from CWC in Muskegon, since no-one in the UK makes the required types.

The Buick and the related Oldsmobile engines made their debuts in small (by American standards) four-door saloons called the Buick Special and Oldsmobile F85. Both proved popular and sold well during the beginning of the new decade, spawning two-door, convertible and even forced-induction versions which widened their appeal considerably. The tuning potential of the lightweight and compact engine was soon recognised, and the 'Aluminum Fireball V8' performed well in stock car races across the country.

Unfortunately, the inexperience of the average American motorist (and, more significantly perhaps, the neighbourhood mechanic) in dealing with aluminium engines soon began to take its toll. Any owner of a Rover V8-engined car today knows the importance of using the correct type and concentration of coolant additive in order to avoid inter-metallic corrosion between the iron and aluminium engine components, but in those less knowledgeable early days bad servicing led to engine waterways becoming heavily silted, to engines overheating and heads warping. Furthermore, General Motors had run into serious problems with porosity of the engine castings, due to their use of adapted transmission-casing die-casting machines. What worked well enough for a bell-shaped casting cast vertically was not so effective when casing a V8 engine block on end.

In parallel with this had come dramatic improvements in iron casting techniques, which allowed much thinner castings to be produced, significantly reducing the weight of cast-iron engine blocks. Since cast-iron engines were also much cheaper and simpler to build, the lovely Buick engine's days were clearly numbered. By the end of 1963 when the 1964 Model Year Buicks and Oldsmobiles appeared, the 'Fireball Aluminum V8' was no more.

Left: *The closest production application to that which would eventually appear in the MGB GT V8 was this Range Rover version, introduced in 1970. Note the four-wheel-drive transmission and substantial exhaust manifolds.*
(Dave Wall/Land Rover)

The Rover Connection

It was early in 1964 that the President of Rover's North American operation, J. Bruce McWilliams, discussed with William Martin-Hurst, the British Managing Director of the still staunchly independent Rover company, the need for a new engine for the Rover car range, a necessity which had already been recognised by the company. The Rover 2000 had been successfully launched in 1963, with an all-new body and engine, but the larger Rover saloons still relied upon an ageing and heavy three-litre straight six. Rover would have liked to extend their range with a variety of powerplants, but the majority of their efforts in the 'fifties had been centred on the gas-turbine engine (at one stage intended as motive power for the P6 Rover 2000!). An all-new larger capacity six-cylinder in-line engine (based on the Rover 2000ohc four-cylinder unit) was also developed, but was found to be too long and heavy for the Rover P6.

McWilliams' suggestion was a simple one. Why not consider adopting a suitable small American V8 engine, which could no doubt be acquired cheaply, would save Rover considerable research and development costs and would aid service costs in the US market? William Martin-Hurst was receptive to this idea, so when he visited the United States to discuss the possibility of selling Rover engines to Mercury Marine, it was natural that he should be on the look-out for an engine which might fulfil Rover's future passenger car requirements.

In Mercury Marine's experimental workshop was an example of the Buick alloy engine, and Martin-Hurst was intrigued to learn more about this neat and compact unit. He found that it would fit easily into the existing engine bay of the Rover P6 — yet it had a capacity of over 3.5 litres — so once he learnt that General Motors were abandoning the engine, Martin-Hurst contacted Ed Rollert of Buick to discuss the possibility of obtaining a licence to build it in Britain.

Despite an initial scepticism about the seriousness of the enquiry, GM management were eventually convinced and the deal was done. GM had already taken the engine out of production, and their high-volume production techniques were in any case inappropriate for Rover, but the new arrangement did include access to all the engineering design drawings, service records and other material. One disadvantage was the fact that the final production versions of the Buick engine differed from the original design drawings, many minor but significant alterations having taken place in course of production. Fortunately, Rover were able to acquire the help of Buick's Chief Engine Designer, Joe Turlay (affectionately nicknamed 'Aluminum Joe' by Rover staff), who was on the point of retiring.

The 'Roverisation' of the engine involved a number of significant alterations, though its basic 215-cubic inch capacity remained unchanged. Rover had no experience with or need for GM-style high-volume engine diecasting facilities, and so the blocks and heads were revised to allow them to be conventionally gravity diecast by Birmingham Aluminium at Smethwick. A further important change was the improvement of the engine's revving capabilities, for despite the strong five-bearing crankshaft and the excellent breathing possibilities inherent in the layout, Rover discovered that there were unacceptable stresses induced in the pistons and valve gear at engine speeds above 4800rpm.

The American Rochester carburettor set-up was dropped in favour of the more familiar twin semi-down-draught SUs,

Above: J. Bruce McWilliams (left) and Rover's British MD, William Martin-Hurst, pictured at the time of Rover's acquisition of the Buick V8 engine in 1964. (John F. Dugdale)

the now familiar 'pent-roof' set-up being designed specially by David Wall. As Wall recollects, the Rochester carburettors were ditched for two reasons: firstly they were virtually obsolete and secondly they were unsuitable for European use: 'I well recall that the Rochester carburettor used to cut out on heavy cornering'.

In order to adapt the engine for UK manufacture, Rover also changed the rocker covers from pressed steel to diecast aluminium, fitted a Lucas distributor and alternator and specially designed exhaust manifolding. The original Rover V8 engines developed some 150bhp gross at 4400rpm, but by the middle of 1967, with the combination of twin carburettors and a lower compression ratio, this had risen to 160bhp gross. By the time the engine appeared in the P6B Rover 3500 in 1968, the engine power was up to 164bhp gross at 5250rpm with outstanding reliability and very long life. (According to David Wall, the SD1 engine of 1976 would originally have peaked at 6250rpm, but for various reasons, not least the oil crisis, the engine that eventually emerged peaked at 5500rpm.)

In the process of revamping the Buick design, new pistons and different materials for valve train, bearing inserts and crankshaft were adopted, resulting in a unit far better suited to European driving practices. David Wall is keen to emphasise that although Rover refined the engine in terms of reliability, the Americans retained the edge when it came to installation refinement; he recalls Joe Turlay saying to him, 'If you can see it, hear it, smell it or feel it, then, boy, you've failed!'. Wall subscribes to the maxim that a pound of felt is worth a ton of theory!

The Rover V8 made its debut in the P5 saloon (which was rechristened the P5B in recognition of the Buick origins of the engine) alongside the MGC at the October 1967 Motor Show, replacing the old three-litre straight six and catapulting the big Rover saloon into an all-new performance sector.

Left: *The Daimler V8 engine was considered as a means of producing a more powerful MGB in 1967, following the BMC/Jaguar merger, but it was soon found to be a poor fit which would have required major surgery to the MGB engine bay and front suspension. This later private conversion, dating from the mid-1970s, shows how difficult such an installation was. (Colin Groves)*

Above: *The purposeful appearance of the Costello B V8 was a selling point in itself, quite apart from the potent performance the car offered. This car, which was tested by Autocar in May 1972, features optional alloy wheels resembling those eventually adopted by MG for their own V8. (Autocar)*

Right: *This early Costello B GT V8 does not feature the familiar 'egg-box' Costello radiator grille and retains the normal MGB Rostyle wheels. (Autosport)*

24

3

Genesis Of
The MGB GT V8

First Ideas and Experiments

The poor response to the MGC might well have put an end to the concept of the larger-engined MG sports car altogether; it was, after all, an area in which the marque had not competed since before the war. Fortunately, however, the merger between Leyland and British Motor Holdings in 1968 brought the Rover and MG marques under the same umbrella, and the idea of a possible marriage between the lightweight and compact Rover V8 and the MG body was soon being contemplated. But there were a few other routes which were investigated beforehand.

The MGC debacle had not only damaged MG's standing (even though the principal problems had not been of Abingdon's making), but had strengthened the hand of the Triumph-dominated senior management in the new British Leyland organisation, which meant that the development of another big-engined MG would have to be carried out on what would nowadays be regarded as a ludicrously tight budget. For example, any engineering changes to the basic MGB structure would have to be of the absolute minimum, so major alterations to the fabric of the MGB body were out of the question.

In the press release issued at the time of the V8 model's launch, British Leyland stated that their marketing team had been studying the sports car market closely during the previous five years and had identified three important facts. They had found that popular sports cars, updated as necessary, usually stayed in production much longer than family cars (a matter of financial necessity, if nothing else), and that a large share of the sports car market was being taken by sports coupé ranges structured to give a wide choice of trims and engines — their way of admitting that Ford's Capri was doing well.

Their final observation was that there was a growing trend towards sports cars with larger engines. Strong contenders in this market sector included not only the Capri but also significant offerings from Datsun, Alfa Romeo and of course Triumph, whose TR6 and Stag models broadly fitted into this picture.

Triumph, with its stronger support in the British Leyland management structure, was allocated funds to investigate a possible range of new sports cars which could, it was felt, eventually replace the whole of the existing MG and Triumph ranges. MG, meanwhile, had to be content to pursue their own ideas at a much more modest level.

✧

The MGB was designed from the outset to accept a family of wide V-form engines which were ultimately stillborn, as well as a straight six-engined derivative, so the engine bay of the basic MGB monocoque was clearly well placed to be able to accept a wide variety of power-plants from elsewhere in the British Leyland organisation.

Mike Twite, in a less than enthusiastic preview report on the MGC in the May 1968 issue of the US magazine *Car & Driver*, concluded his article with the statement that '…somewhere deep within the MG works is an MGB with the 2.5-litre Coventry Climax V8'. Although this was probably a little off the mark, it does perhaps hint that MG were already concerned about the MGC, even at that early stage.

MG authority Mike Allison, who was working at the factory at the time, recalls Terry Mitchell investigating the possibility of using the smooth and well-engineered Ed Turner-designed Daimler 2.5-litre V8 engine in the MGB, once the BMC/Jaguar merger had taken place: a bodyshell was mounted on the inspection table and a bare engine and gearbox were dropped in. However, it soon became apparent that the engine layout was not very suitable and the body and chassis members would have required considerable modification, which financial constraints had already ruled out. There were doubts, in any case, about both the suitability and the long-term future of the engine.

Parallel work involved the investigation of the larger 4.5-litre Daimler Majestic Major V8, but again the physical size of the engine soon put paid to this idea. Bob Neville, working in the Development Shop at the time, remembers a blue MGB tourer being cut in half and the halves moved apart in an attempt to fit the Daimler unit. Terry Mitchell subsequently pointed out to the author that the Daimler unit would have required significant redesign of the front suspension (shades of the MGC!), so the scheme was doomed from the outset; with the Leyland merger of the following year, all such schemes were in any case put back into the melting pot.

Interestingly, a Daimler V8-engined MGB roadster was built in the early 1970's by an employee of the well-known Ricardo engineering consultancy, using the company's facilities but working in his own time. This car — which the owner called 'LeMans 51A' — survives to this day. There was no official Abingdon, Ricardo or Daimler participation in the project, but it remains an interesting illustration of what might have been.

✧

Ken Costello and the Costello V8

Ken Costello is now twenty-five years older than when he built his first MGB V8 conversion, but the twinkle in his eye and his youthful enthusiasm for his work are as vivid as ever. In the 1960s he made a name for himself as a successful Mini racer, featuring often in the pages of such magazines as *Cars & Car Conversions*, where the Mini racing scene was avidly followed. Yet despite his success with small-engined cars, Ken held by the maxim that 'there's no substitute for cubic inches' when he took on his first MGB V8 conversion.

The car in question was a red MGB roadster, which he built between June and November 1969. It featured an Oldsmobile engine, which differed slightly from the Buick version in having an extra set of studs in the head and superior combustion chambers. A year later, the first car built for a customer was delivered, and before very long people were beating a path to his premises in Farnborough, Kent, and asking for replicas. Ken never spent much money promoting the car (though the author does seems to recall seeing an advertisement in a contemporary issue of either *Autocar* or *Motor*). However, he was astute enough to ask several motoring correspondents to try it out, including Gordon Wilkins (*The Observer*) and John Langley (*The Daily Telegraph*); following their favourable comments, the car became so constantly in demand that Ken found himself building one or two a week — a remarkable achievement for such a small enterprise, even more so when one considers that the cost of the conversion was around 50 percent up on that of the base car.

Ken eventually converted in excess of 200 MGBs. The initial conversion comprised an MGB (or GT) monocoque, into which he squeezed a standard 150bhp Rover P6 engine, complete with the Dave Wall-designed pentroof SU carburettor set up, which he mated to the standard MGB gearbox but with a 9.5in diameter clutch in a special bell housing. Drive was then transmitted to the standard MGB type rear axle, although the final drive ratio was altered to that of the MGC (3.07:1), which was the same ratio MG would later use for their own V8.

The Rover P6 carburettor installation sat high in the central vee of the engine, unable to fit under the low MGB bonnet. Ken's solution was to fabricate a glassfibre reinforced substitute bonnet with a large teardrop-shaped bulge in the centre. At the same time, he did away with the small central plinth at the bonnet's edge (a feature which BL had retained for reasons of economy) and replaced the rather bland recessed grille of the contemporary MGB with his own 'egg-box' grille, specially fabricated in aluminium.

The combination of the new bonnet and the special Costello grille gave the car a distinctive appearance which set it apart from humbler MGBs in a way that the subsequent factory car was never able to achieve. Aided further by the neat 'V-Eight Costello' tail-badge and the chunky alloy wheels fitted to many conversions, the car had a mean, purposeful look, in keeping with its performance potential.

The enthusiasm generated by the Costello conversions was such that it was soon common knowledge within the motoring fraternity — including the senior management at British Leyland. According to Ken, 'Charles Griffin of BL wrote to me and asked if he could see one of my cars', and shortly thereafter a Costello V8 was driven by Griffin, with Harry Webster and George Turnbull in attendance. Two weeks later, Costello took one to Berkeley Square for Lord Stokes to see. 'What would you do if we made one of these ourselves?'Stokes asked him. Ken replied that it would take the company two years to put it into production, so he would just carry on building them. Requested by BL to convert a car for them to assess, Ken produced a left-hand-drive Harvest Gold GT using a new car and Rover engine supplied by the company. Don Hayter, in an interview with motoring journalist Chris Goffey, remembered examining it: 'There was a welded joint in the steering column, which we could not have tolerated, and the steering joint was very close to the exhaust manifold; there was only about an eighth of an inch clearance. There was about twice the torque of the standard car, so you could get quite violent axle tramp if you accelerated hard.' Nevertheless, the Abingdon team were understandably enthusiastic about the prospect of being allowed to build such a car themselves and, once given the go-ahead, they had their prototype up and running in no time. Ken Costello is defensive of the spliced and welded steering joint: 'We tested every single example to 140 lb ft torque and when we did try to break one, the column twisted before the joint could break'.

In May 1972, about a year after the Abingdon engineers had examined one of his cars, Ken Costello was invited by *Autocar* magazine to submit a Costello V8 for a road-test feature. The car made a strongly favourable impression: the full-blown 'Auto-Test' which appeared in the May 25 issue included a comprehensive and impressive set of performance figures, and prompted the observation: 'We can think of no reason why BLMC are not producing it themselves, and their product planners ought to be ashamed at not having spotted this potential market.'

As installed in the Costello car, the ex-Rover P6 engine produced 58 percent more power than the contemporary four-cylinder B-series engine and a whopping 80 percent more torque. *Autocar* found that they could accelerate the car up to 40mph in first gear before the hydraulic tappets pumped up at high engine revs, although the V8 was at its best as a smooth, powerful unit providing effortless acceleration at a twitch of the accelerator, without the constant need to stir the gearbox. In the light of Don Hayter's comments, it is interesting that *Autocar* found no trace of axle tramp, which suggests that either the *Autocar* V8 was better set up or the springs on the earlier car were tired.

Summing up, *Autocar* noted that the main drawback of the car was its outdated MGB cabin: 'MGB owners will have come to terms with all this, but anyone expecting this car to be as well planned and equipped as, say, a Datsun 240Z, will be disappointed. That is British Leyland's fault, not Ken Costello's.'

Within a couple of weeks of the *Autocar* piece, their rivals at *Motor* magazine carried out their own test, though this time using a customer car, registered NLC 366K. Their verdict was similarly enthusiastic, but in their report they observed that 'rumour has it that Ken won't be the only man in the MGB V8 conversion business for very much longer'. By June 1973, the factory car was only a couple of months from launch, and its development had in certain quarters become something of an open secret. *Motor*'s reported 0-60mph time was down slightly on *Autocar*'s, 8.0 seconds as against 7.8, but the situation was reversed when they quoted their top gear 30-50mph time: they claimed 5.6 seconds, whereas *Autocar* had achieved 5.8. What was clear from both magazines' results was that the figures were phenomenal in comparison with those for the contemporary four-cylinder car, which could only manage around 11.6 seconds 0-60mph and 8.8 seconds 30-50mph — around three seconds slower than each of the comparable Costello figures.

By the summer of 1973, Ken had revised the specification of his cars, including the substitution of a different carburettor installation which did away with the need for a bonnet bulge, although the distinctive Costello 'egg-box' grille was still available as an alternative to the 1972 MGB facelift grille. These later cars were designated 'Costello MGB V8 Mark II', and because they were soon overtaken by the factory MGB GT V8 (launched in August) they are consequently very much rarer. Just two weeks before the official MGB GT V8 was launched, Ken cheekily placed a half-page advertisement in *Autocar* which warned the reader to 'beware of imitations'!

The factory car understandably put a large dent in Ken's business; so did British Leyland's decision to stop supplying him directly with engines. An edict issued by BL to their dealers ordered them not to sell any Rover V8 engines without taking a unit in part exchange, thus almost eliminating the supply of brand-new units. Ken responded by importing Buick and Oldsmobile units from scrapped cars in Belgium ('we brought 40 back in one go on one occasion'), and these engines were then stripped and placed in an acid bath before rebuilding with new Rover innards.

Just the same, the factory V8 cut deeply into Costello's business and even after it was dropped in 1976 cars emerged from his workshops in only a trickle. It is important to note that a number of Costello imitations were built during the 1970s, cashing in on the Costello name but possessing none of the engineering integrity of the originals. Some of these cars even used genuine Costello parts and have occasionally resulted in unfair allegations of poor quality in the real thing.

To this day, Ken Costello's fame rests almost wholly on his introduction of the V8 unit into the MGB. As we shall see further on, however, the connection between man and car was by no means over.

Top: An early Costello GT V8, owned by V8 Register member Mark Vine. Compare this view with the photograph of the Rover P5B saloon engine bay in Chapter Two. (Mark Vine)

Above: The Abingdon Development team were instructed to examine a Costello car and carry out an engineering assessment of it. This view shows the underside of the lhd car Costello built for them. Don Hayter pointed out to the author the proximity of the exhaust to both the flexible clutch hose and the solenoid wiring. The Costello car also retained the standard MGB gearbox. (Don Hayter).

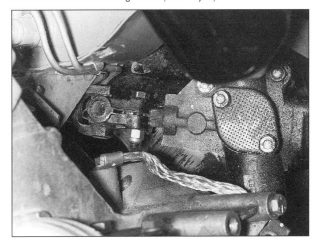

Right: Costello tried to solve the problem of limited underbonnet space by modifying the steering column to incorporate two universal joints which he cut, spliced and welded to the original column shaft. This close-up factory shot shows the lower Torrington joint adjacent to the rack itself. (Don Hayter)

Above: The engine bay of the V8 built by Costello for British Leyland. At this stage, Abingdon were still very much keeping in mind the possibility of export to the USA (hence the left-hand-drive configuration) and Don Hayter noted on the back of this picture that there would be a problem finding space for the air pump necessary to comply with US exhaust emmissions legislations. (Don Hayter)

Above: This detail shot of the Costello/Leyland V8 shows the upper steering joint, which Don Hayter remarks was too close to the exhaust manifold, even with the special allen screw-head bolt which Costello used. (Don Hayter)

Another interesting but abortive experiment was carried out by Geoff Healey at the Healey's Warwick works, in the form of an MGB GT fitted with the small but high-revving Coventry Climax 1.8-litre V8. Don Hayter recalls visiting the 'Cinema' at Warwick (the Healey works were situated in a former cinema), along with Syd Enever, and seeing this car. Although the Climax-engined MGB was never likely to have been a serious candidate for production, it was an interesting exercise. Hayter remembers that the Coventry Climax unit sat very low and neatly between the chassis side members, which necessitated very tight specially fabricated exhaust manifolds, similar to those adopted in later years by many MGB V8 converters.

The Healeys had built up a good working relationship with the Coventry Climax company over the years, even before they came under the wing of the same organisation when British Motor Holdings was formed: several Healey projects used Coventry Climax units. In his second volume of Healey history, *More Healeys*, Geoff Healey recalls that the company investigated the possibility of a 2.5-litre Coventry Climax V8-engined successor to the Austin-Healey 3000, which would have used a Jaguar gearbox. However, Coventry Climax was deprived of its engine development and production facility even before the Leyland merger, reverting to the production of fork-lift trucks, so the V8-engined Big Healey replacement and, by inference, the Coventry Climax MGB, were both immediately rendered redundant.

The project which was always likely to be a more realistic prospect for production was the installation of the Rover alloy V8. Certainly, as soon as Rover and MG became part of the same organisation, the Abingdon team became strongly enthusiastic about the possibilities. In the rival Rootes camp, the Sunbeam Alpine had been successfully transformed into the potent Sunbeam Tiger road-burner simply by shoehorning an American Ford 4.7-litre V8 engine under the bonnet, so the attraction of a similar exercise with the American designed Buick/Rover unit was obvious.

John Thornley remembers that early overtures from Abingdon to their Longbridge masters fell on stony ground, ostensibly because the Rover V8 engines were being allocated to their full capacity. As Thornley recalls: 'We were told that the total permissible output was bespoke; for the Rover, for the Range Rover, and some other fringe uses. But MG got hold of an engine and design work associated with its installation went on, albeit somewhat surreptitiously! About this time Costello was converting MGBs to V8s (maybe one of the 'fringe uses'!) and in due time this was noticed by the top brass who wanted to know why Abingdon were not making one. The door for the supply of engines was opened and everybody was astonished at how quickly a prototype was produced.'

The First Prototype

The intense interest aroused by the Costello cars led to his being asked to produce an example for MG to study, which he duly did. Reactions at Abingdon were mixed: former Development Foreman Cliff Bray remembers that 'the conversion was perhaps not too bad considering the resources which were available to Costello in comparison to ours', but there were a number of features which did not impress the MG team. In order to get round the problem of clearance to the steering column (a difficulty re-experienced 20 years later

with the RV8 development cars), Costello had spliced in a welded universal joint, which MG frowned upon; and the transplant used the normal Rover P6 engine which necessitated the distinctive Costello bonnet bulge.

At the same time, August 1971, instructions came from Longbridge for MG to build a running prototype themselves, a task which MG Chief Engineer Roy Brocklehurst passed to Chief Chassis Engineer Terry Mitchell, assisted by his team of Barry Jackson, Bob Staniland, Ron Lindars and Pat Rees. Mitchell recalls coming back from holiday on August the fourth and Brocklehurst emerging from his office to tell him, 'We've got to put a Rover V8 in the MGB', a project which was immediately assigned the Abingdon experimental code of EX249 — 'ADO23 — Rover V8'. The EX-Register itself shows the first drawing entry — drawing number EX249/1 for the clutch scheme — as being dated August 5 1971, which shows just how quickly Mitchell and his team got down to work.

The team took a Rover P6 unit and a Midnight Blue MGB GT shell and created the prototype in just four weeks. (One of Mitchell's instructions during those weeks was that if anyone rang him up, he was 'not available'.) At the end of that

intense period, not only had the car itself been built but the appropriate drawings had been prepared (the last one in the series, EX249/104, being dated September 4), and the whole package was ready for inspection by senior engineering and management personnel. Harry Webster was among those who came from Longbridge to look at the car, and Mitchell was disappointed that he passed up the chance to drive it.

Work by the development team had resulted in a lowered engine which reduced the clearance problems of the Abingdon car by comparison with Costello's. Even so, the prototype retained the standard Rover P6 carburettor arrangement, necessitating two neat tear-drop shaped bulges in the bonnet which, as recorded elsewhere in this chapter, reminded Geoff Allen of a certain 'prominent' young lady of the time! And there were other alterations necessitated by clearance problems in the engine bay, such as the remote oil filter and a relocated steering rack.

Terry Mitchell recalls with a chuckle that the normal Rover P6 oil pump as installed in the prototype originally gave only about six psi pressure at idle, so the system was redesigned to overcome that rather obvious flaw!

Abingdon Gets The Go-Ahead

Harry Webster was sufficiently impressed by the Mitchell prototype that permission was given to develop the car for production, under the Austin Drawing Office code of ADO75. Development work continued throughout the autumn and winter of 1971, with the intention of a launch in the latter half of 1972. In the event, the launch was postponed, but by the end of 1972 pre-production cars were being built and the V8's public debut was re-scheduled for summer 1973, by which time, as verified by the ADO drawing-register, 439 drawings had been produced by MG alone!

Although a roadster version was deemed feasible (even though some people at Abingdon harboured a suspicion that scuttle shake might have been a problem, particularly since they had had to fit a cross tube beneath the dashboard in the original MGB to alleviate such problems), the decision was taken to proceed with the GT version alone and no roadster prototype was built.

Engine Changes

It was Alec Hounslow, former racing mechanic to Nuvolari and by the early 'seventies MG's development department foreman, who came up with the inspired inlet manifold arrangement whereby the twin SU HIF6 (Horizontal Integral Float Chamber) carburettors were mounted transversely behind the engine, just in front of the heater box. This installation, engineered by Hounslow in conjunction with Henry Stone, was found by the MG engineers to give a reduced temperature scatter from one cylinder to another in comparison with the conventional Rover pent-roof installation. (It was also examined by Rover at Solihull, where David Wall and his team carried out mixture distribution checks on their test bed and found that the MG set-up was inferior to that of the contemporary Rover P6B; clearly there was some disagreement between Abingdon and Solihull as to who was right in this matter.)

To provide air for the rear-mounted carburettors, Hounslow devised the distinctive MGB GT V8 'lobster claw' air intake arrangements, incorporating neat bi-metallic valves (an award-winning Austin Morris invention) which could draw

Above: Fitted to all factory V8s, the composite Dunlop wheel comprised a machined cast alloy centre riveted to a chrome plated steel rim. Note also the standard fit Goodyear G800 HR rated tyre. Compare this wheel with the similarly styled alloy wheel fitted to the Autocar road test Costello V8, pictured earlier in this chapter. (What Car?)

Below: The V8 badge at the front end of the car was borrowed from the contemporary Rover saloons. (Rover)

TERRY MITCHELL

Terry Mitchell spent almost thirty years with the MG Car Company, working his way up from novice draughtsman to Chief Chassis Engineer. Along the way he participated in a wonderful variety of projects which were fundamental to postwar MG history. Terry was born in 1921, and like many of his generation was inspired during boyhood by Meccano sets and steam engines. The latter remain to this day one of his major interests.

On leaving school, Terry was keen to work in the drawing office at the Great Western Railway's Swindon works, but this was not to be; instead, he sat the appropriate exam at Paddington and in April 1937 started as a junior clerk at Maidenhead station. Following a spell of wartime service as a flight mechanic and fitter in the RAF, there were a couple of unmemorable jobs — one of them as a draughtsman with a milking-plant company — before in 1950 he spotted an advertisement for a position in the Cowley-based MG & Riley drawing-office.

Interviewed by Gerald Palmer, the gifted engineer/stylist who had himself only recently joined MG's parent Nuffield organisation from Jowett, he made a sufficiently good impression to be offered the job at once. By a stroke of good fortune, he began his Cowley career at a drawing-board next to that of a gifted graduate named Tom Honeysett, whose guidance was very much needed during such early projects as adapting the existing Riley RME & RMA models to take hydraulic brakes, and designing and detailing the rear suspension for the Riley Pathfinder.

These tasks involved a great deal of research and investigation by the novice Mitchell, including the detailed interpretation of masses of Riley drawings, and the experience stood him in good stead for the challenges which arose later in his career. Work was not confined to the drawing office, however: 'I can recall driving around the countryside on a bare Pathfinder chassis which had been weighted down with brake drums to simulate the body weight. It was an education, watching the full range of suspension movements from the driving position!'

In addition to the Riley Pathfinder (which Terry still asserts was a much-maligned car) the Cowley drawing-office staff were responsible for much of the work carried out on the ZA Magnette and of course the TF Midget, although Terry describes the latter as little more than a 'knife and fork' styling job. Syd Enever was naturally a regular visitor at Cowley, and when the Abingdon drawing-office was established in 1954 Terry was requested to re-locate there, to which he happily agreed. His first project at the new location was the body of the EX179 Record Breaker. Syd Enever's instructions were for a body which 'looked just like EX135 (the prewar record breaker) but different' — apparently a typical Enever brief! Later, in collaboration with Enever, Terry designed the distinctive tapered body of EX181 — known to the media as the 'Roaring Raindrop' — the lines of which would serve as inspiration for the MGB roadster. During the years which followed Terry was closely involved in virtually all significant MG development work, including of course the MGA and MGB. (He also remembers a surreptitiously developed Le Mans prototype, EX186, on which Dickie Wright did most of the draugh-

Terry Mitchell, pictured at his Abingdon home in 1993. (David Knowles)

ting work, which had to be hurriedly disposed of when the powers at BMC got wind of it. 'John Thornley told us to crate it up and get rid of it. I think it was shipped to San Francisco.')

By the early 1970s, Terry had risen to the rank of Chief Chassis Engineer, second in command to Chief Engineer Roy Brocklehurst. Supervising the building of the first official MGB GT V8 prototype was a task which he recalls as among the most pleasant of his career, particularly as he was able to get on with it unburdened by interruptions or peripheral problems. Like most of his contemporaries at Abingdon, Terry recalls the V8 car with great affection, mingled with sadness and a little bitterness that it was never given the opportunity it deserved. He was also involved in the mid-engined ADO 21 prototype, which was seen by some at Abingdon as the great hope for MG's future, but which came to nothing.

Terry's final job, in conjunction with Jim O'Neill, was to translate the Honda drawings for the 'Bounty' project — a task which quickly soured when he learnt that the production car was to carry the Triumph badge. Following the closure of the factory, Terry was able to return to his first love — model steam locomotives. Typically, he not only has his own garden railway, but is building an exquisitely detailed one-eighth-scale steam locomotive, for which the standards of drawing and assembly are characteristically high.

Above: *The dashboard of one of the MGB GT V8 Press Cars, tested by What Car? magazine in their first issue. Note the 60psi oil pressure gauge and round choke knob, both of which were later changed, and the layout of the minor switch-gear on the central console (below the radio) which was reversed on all subsequent production cars. (What Car?)*

Below: *The fact that this is a very early MGB GT V8 is shown by the radiator fan guard and the extra clips at the rear of the air filters. The throttle cable has been incorrectly fitted beneath the off-side air filter. (What Car?)*

warm air for the carburettors from sleeves fitted around the exhaust manifolds. This speeded the 'warming up' period, but allowed cooler air to be drawn in once the engine *had* warmed up.

The exhaust manifold arrangement was designed by Barry Jackson and mocked up in steel by Brian 'Bunny' Hillier (now with the Williams racing team), an ace fabricator who was able to knock up a fabricated steel manifold arrangement in double-quick time. Terry Mitchell pointed out that the rectangular section of these manifolds where they led into the downpipes was necessitated by the tight clearance to the MGB engine bay chassis frame members: 'Ideally we would have liked to have moved these members out by about an inch, but that would have cost money, which was of course out of the question.' Nevertheless, the installation was successful, clearing the way for the testing of the car in North Wales by MG's test driver, Tommy Haig.

Even though this arrangement obviated the need for any bonnet bulges, the clearances were sufficiently tight that it was decided as a precautionary measure to retool the MGB bonnet

to provide a slightly sharper curvature, and hence greater clearance. The construction of the all-alloy Rover V8 engine meant that despite its significantly larger capacity and much higher power and torque outputs, the basic engine itself was some 40lbs lighter than the contemporary 1798 cc B-series four-cylinder unit. Despite this, the ancillary equipment fitted resulted in a slight increase in overall weight. The front to rear ratio of the MGB GT V8 was 49.4/50.6 percent compared with the 47.8/52.2 percent ratio of the four-cylinder model.

Gearbox

The gearbox used for the MGB GT V8 was the same basic unit which had been introduced for the MGC in 1968, but with a different clutch and bell-housing in order to mate with the Rover engine. MGB and MGC models with overdrive always had this facility on third and top gear, and this was originally intended for the V8 as well. However, it soon became apparent that the massive torque reversals which occurred when switching in and out of overdrive third could lead to dramatic failure of the gearbox, and indeed the gearbox was a noted weak spot of the car even without that problem.

It was therefore decided to modify the gear selector mechanism so that overdrive third was blanked out, and overdrive was restricted to fourth as a 'cruising' ratio. However, despite this, a number of cars slipped through with overdrive on third and although it is difficult to be certain how many it appears to have been quite a number.

The clutch of the V8 was enlarged, and the relative refinement of a roller-bearing clutch release bearing was added (the MGB had to make do with a carbon surfaced bearing). British Leyland already had some experience of the roller-bearing clutch release with the Austin Maxi, and said as much in the MGB GT V8 Press Release, but the remainder of the Maxi's transmission train was hardly worthy of great pride!

Body Styling and Trim

As we have seen, the development of the MGB GT V8 was a fairly rushed and extremely budget-conscious affair: British Leyland had other more pressing matters to attend to than the launch of a new MG sports car, and any budget allocated for sports car development was either being spent on meeting the requirement of export market legislation or was going to Triumph. Consequently, the people responsible for the appearance of the car were working within narrow limits.

The autumn of 1972 had seen a facelift of the MGB and MGB GT range, following representations and a suggestion from J. Bruce McWilliams of Leonia, New Jersey, which brought back the attractive grille casing of the 1962-68 MGB but with a black plastic cross-mesh grille instead of the vertical chrome slats of the original. The MG shield badge was once more proudly mounted in front of the small raised plinth at the leading edge of the bonnet — a happy reversion to the original MGB since it had looked so totally inappropriate on the recessed-grille car introduced in 1969. Previous attempts to improve the front of the MGB had met with no success, and for the V8 none was seriously considered other than the mounting of a small 'V8' badge on the nearside half of the grille. Far more important, at any rate, was the matter of the 'Costello bonnet-bulge' and its solution.

The Abingdon team were similarly restricted when it came to upgrading the interior, an area already much criticised by motoring writers in their assessments of the much cheaper original MGB. Given the market sector in which the V8 was expected to compete, it is not at all surprising that its interior trim was regarded as a distinct let-down: the dashboard largely retained the same crinkle-finish steel as was to be found in the MGB (though with smaller main instruments, adopted in order to accommodate a collapsible steering column assembly), and the only other change was the standard fitting of head re-straints and tinted window glass, both of which were available as options on the smaller-engined car. (Significantly, for the RV8 Rover would specify an attractive walnut fascia and leather upholstery, features which many pundits felt belonged in the first V8 and which are popular nowadays for those seeking to improve their cars.)

Much criticism was directed at the MGB GT V8 for not looking 'different' enough. It was a verdict for which its creators, given their lack of means, could hardly be blamed.

Suspension and Brakes

Ideally, the Abingdon engineers would have been able to carry out a thorough reworking of the MGB suspension for the V8; but, once again, budgetary constraints worked against them. The MGC had featured a totally redesigned (torsion bar) front suspension, due to the need to accommodate the vast three-litre straight six, but that set-up had been abandoned along with the car and its re-introduction was not economically viable.

Roy Brocklehurst devised a scheme which would have provided an 'A'-frame rear radius arm set up to provide better location for the back axle, whilst retaining the leaf springs. Such a set-up had been employed on the SSV1 Safety Car (of which

Above: *Tom Studer of Switzerland is the enthusiastic owner of this US Development car, chassis number GD2D2-DUD-109G. He has extensively researched all the lhd cars, all of which survive. (Tom Studer/Motorsport-Fotos)*

Below: *Eric Prasse of Switzerland owns this lhd pre-production V8, seen here at a Swiss MG Car Club event. (Tom Studer)*

Above: Geoff Allen pictured with the first production rubber-bumper MGB GT V8, GD2D1-2101G, which is owned by his wife Jean. (Popular Classics)

Above: Also resident in Switzerland, this is the first lhd production V8, GD2D2-DUD-101G. Here it is seen in the V8 Register compound at the MG Car Club's annual Silverstone International weekend, 1993. (David Knowles)

Below: US specification MGB's of the 1970s were distinguished by this chassis plate affixed to the driver's side door sill. Date of manufacture is December 1972; chassis number is GD2D2-DUD-102G, identifying this as the Glacier white car now owned by Bas Geritts and featured in the colour pages of this book. (Bas Geritts)

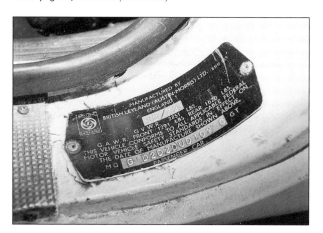

Recollections of MGB GT V8

Production At Abingdon

by Geoff Allen

Although we knew of Ken Costello's conversions, my first realisation of the possibility of an Abingdon factory-built version of the MGB V8 was when I saw and heard an MGB with a bonnet with two bulges in a position which gave the impression that Sabrina Duncan had been shut inside. (Anyone under 45 will not know who she was, but suffice to say her main attributes lay in front of her!)

After this, the tendency was to listen for any 'Bs coming out of the Development Department, as by this time tarpaulin screens had been fitted to the top of the partition wall between Rectification and Development This was meant to prevent us worthies in the Rectification Shop standing on the benches to peer over the top at anything a bit unusual in the Development Shop, which was next to us in the same block.

We did hear bits and pieces about modifications to get the Rover carburettors to fit under the bonnet of the 'B without necessitating the aforementioned bulges, and after a while we heard the unmistakeable V8 exhaust note coming from cars with standard bonnets fitted. These cars, we learned later, were fitted with the now familiar induction manifolding set-up, designed by Alec Hounslow.

In the early 1970s, I was alternating between electrical and mechanical work in the Rectification Shop, as the need arose. One day I was asked to go into Paint Finishing and get a V8 and bring it round to Rectification. This was a left-hand-drive car painted in the attractive dark Mallard Green colour, and was the first of many V8s I was to work on, both in the factory and following its closure. I can well remember starting it, putting it into gear and promptly stalling the engine, at which some wag remarked, 'I would have thought you could have kept it running with all those cylinders.' (He must have been a visitor; our lot weren't like that!)

The seven cars to the proposed North American specification were about in early 1973, and we did work on them at various times. I remember, for example, changing the speedometers from kph to mph on two cars, one of which was the Green Mallard car GD2D1-101G, the first production V8. It was said that they were destined for the New York Motor Show, but where they actually went after that I do not recall. These cars were mounted on the line during December 1972 and January 1973, with one home-market specification car also in January. No V8s were mounted in February 1973 and very few in March or April, and so it was not until May 1973 that production reached over 100 per month, peaking at 188 in October but thereafter dropping considerably; in fact, production of 100 cars per month was only achieved four times before and seven times after October 1973.

(Geoff Allen's recollections continue in Chapter Four.)

more below) although that car, with Automotive Products' advanced anti-roll suspension system, had employed rear coil springs. Roy, however, moved to Longbridge (where he was to work on the ADO88/LC8 Metro and the LC10 Maestro) prior to the launch of the V8, and work on the car devolved to others at Abingdon. Sadly the improved suspension, which would have made a substantial difference to the handling of the car, was never sanctioned and MG had to make do with stiffer springs, similar to those specified for police MGBs.

The brakes of the V8 were of critical importance, since the car was capable of much greater speeds than its four-cylinder sister. The basic set-up of the MGB was retained and MG resorted to thicker front discs with what was effectively an amalgam of MGB and Triumph 2500 calliper halves. At the rear, the MGB roadster brake slave cylinder was used in the interest of better balanced braking.

Wheels and Tyres

In 1970, the Foleshill, Coventry-based Dunlop Wheels Division began to market a number of styled alloy and composite steel/alloy wheels in their 'Formula D' range. These attractively styled wheels were soon seen on a variety of cars including Ford Escorts, Austin 1300GTs and others, although they were usually sold through the car accessory market rather than being supplied as standard equipment or factory-fitted options. One of the range, the 'D4' wheel, comprised cast alloy wheel centres (in a choice of three styles) riveted to chrome plated steel rims. In testing, these wheels proved remarkably durable and strong and were a natural choice for Dunlop to use as the basis for the first prototypes of what would eventually become their 'Denovo' run-flat safety tyre.

The late 'sixties and early 'seventies had seen a growth in public awareness of vehicle safety, exemplified by American consumer activist Ralph Nader's persistent lobbying in the USA which had led to the demise of Chevrolet's rear-engine Corvair. In this climate, the stage was set for an exhibition of safety vehicle systems in Washington DC in the spring of 1972, at which MG exhibited their own proposal (coded EX250) in the form of 'SSV1' or 'Safety Systems Vehicle One', based on an MGB GT and featuring, among many other novel features, the Dunlop wheels (basically 'Formula D4 style B') and run-flat tyres — described as 'Dunlop Total Mobility'.

These wheels (which were also being adopted in slightly different form for the Reliant Scimitar GTE sports estate) were obviously right for the car and were chosen for the MGB GT V8 as a cheap but effective means of setting it apart from its humbler brethren. The Abingdon engineers found that the 5Jx14 V8 wheels were the strongest wheels ever fitted to an MG. In laboratory rig testing, up to 600,000 load reversals were required; in the case of the V8 wheels, the test batch was removed after three million reversals and a single wheel, kept on purely for the sake of interest, was still going strong at six million load reversals!

A further advantage was the standard of production of the Dunlop D4 wheels. As John Thornley recalls: 'To me the great virtue of these wheels was that they were circular and concentric, which is more than could be said of some other types of wheel I could mention!'

Tyres adopted were slightly larger than those of the MGB — 175 section for the V8 rather than the 165 of the four — and were consequently slightly greater in their rolling diameter, a factor which affected the overall gearing ratio. Most early cars were fitted with Goodyear G800 tyres (always HR

Above: Bas Geritts acquired this experimental US emissions V8 engine from V8 Register Committee member Paul Busby and fitted it to his Glacier White car. Note the large air pump at the front of the engine and the air injector tubing plumbed into the cylinder head above each exhaust opening. (Bas Geritts)

rather than SR rated due to the higher top speed of the V8), although Dunlops were also fitted from time to time. To this day, most car manufacturers are reluctant to put all their eggs in one basket!

The Export Development Cars

From the outset, it was the hope of both the MG team at Abingdon and the salesmen in Leonia, New Jersey, that the V8-engined MGB would be exported to MG's most important market. As Don Hayter recalls, J. Bruce McWilliams was very enthusiastic about the car and especially wanted to see a roadster version, which was technically quite feasible and could have been easily engineered if the need had arisen. Mike Allison was responsible at the time for the Air Pollution Control Centre at the MG factory and was involved in the work necessitated to adapt the Rover V8 engine to satisfy US exhaust emissions requirements, including the even more stringent demands of California legislation.

Don Hayter recalls that ten engines were built by Rover's Experimental Department and were coded in the sequence EXP147 upwards — EXP147 itself now resides in Don's own rather special ex-O-series development V8 roadster. EXP148 was later acquired by the V8 Register's Paul Busby and then by Bas Gerrits who fitted it appropriately in his ex-US assessment Glacier White left-hand-drive MGB GT V8.

Seven complete cars with the appropriate GD2D2-DUD chassis number prefixes were built to USA specification. By chance, Mike Allison happened to be in California at the time that the MGB GT V8 was launched in the UK. 'The Americans were delirious about the car, and all the dealers wanted to place orders for it. One actually said that if the TR6's and GT6's were relabelled as MGs they would be easier to sell!' The cars were tested and approved, and both MG and the North American dealers who knew about the car were enthusiastic about its prospects. George Turnbull of Austin Morris accompanied the cars on their trip to America and noted the enthusiasm of the dealers, but sadly the political climate militated against the V8 and destroyed all chance of Americans being able to own and drive them.

Above: Don Hayter (left) on the occasion of the retirement of Alec Hounslow, who had master-minded the unique MGB GT V8 carburettor installation. Behind them are members of the MG Development team, with Chief Chassis Engineer Terry Mitchell at the extreme right. The US-specifcation Midgets in the background date the picture around early 1974. (Don Hayter)

Below: Pictured in 1974 at a gathering for the retirement of secretary Isla Watts (sister of Dougie Watts of Comps) are (left to right) Don Hayter, Syd Enever, Isla Watts and Roy Brocklehurst. Syd Enever was in happy retirement himself by this time and Roy Brocklehurst had moved to Longbridge to work on Austin Morris development, including ADO88 & ADO99. (Don Hayter)

Preliminary plans had called for a production rate for the V8 of around 100 cars per week, of which 50 percent would have gone to the USA, but in the event only half that rate was achieved and as a result of a high-level British Leyland decision the V8 was not exported (even to mainland Europe). As sales literature makes plain, it was obviously still thought that the V8 would be exported at quite a late stage before the actual launch, since mention of the availability of left-hand- drive and kph speedometers was made in the first MGB GT V8 leaflet. The decision not to export the car, more than any other factor, resulted in the dropping of any ideas for a roadster version.

As Roy Brocklehurst said to Wilson McComb in an interview for *Classic Cars* magazine in January 1987: 'Oh, there may have been some thoughts about lack of torsional stiffness, but the real reason for restricting the V8 engine to the GT body was that we reckoned we could sell as many GTs as we could get engines. It was the availability problem that restricted us to the low-compression Range Rover unit — and it was the availability problem that killed the V8 in the end.' There can be little doubt that if circumstances had allowed the exporting of the car to the USA, with the consequent rise in production, a (homologated) roadster version could have been built.

In the end, the cars were returned from the USA and were sold off as they were, emissions equipment and all, to members of the sales and service staff in the company. Through the determined efforts of Swiss V8 Register member Tom Studer, helped by V8 Register Historian Geoff Allen, the subsequent history of each of these seven cars has been traced, and it is nice to be able to record that all of them have survived.

The MGB GT V8 in Production

The Market

Production of the V8 commenced in December 1972, with an intended launch time of summer the following year. In the interim, production totalled about 350 cars, and during the same period British Leyland's Austin Morris sales and marketing division at Longbridge made their own preparations for the launch.

BL targeted the V8 at owners and enthusiasts of the current crop of fairly expensive, low-production, high-performance European sporting coupés. In a letter to dealers dated July the 30th, 1973, the Austin Morris advertising division enclosed three specimen advertisements, including two for insertion by the dealer, complete with his name and address, in appropriate magazines. These advertisements all featured an airbrushed illustration of the V8 front-end on, to be headed by one of two slogans: either 'The new 124mph MGB GT V8 is here' or, more pointedly, 'If you've just bought a Reliant Scimitar GTE, a Datsun 240Z or an Alfa Romeo 2000 GTV, this will ruin your day'. (This direct-challenge slogan was used throughout the national press.) In addition, there was a so-called 'stock block', which was a simple high-contrast black and white drawing of an MGB GT V8 for the dealer to use as part of his own advertising layouts.

Also in July, British Leyland issued press packs to national and motoring publications, which again revealed the company's intention of tackling the mid- to upmarket sports coupé sector.

The Launch and The Press

As soon as the news of a new MG sports car became known to the British motoring press, the race was on between the two leading UK magazines, *Autocar* and *Motor*, to put the car through the rigours of a full road test and judge whether it was worthy of the octagon. The interest among journalists was understandable: although the last big-engined MG had in their eyes been a monumental flop, their reporting of the Costello-converted V8 had clearly indicated the marvellous potential of a full factory conversion.

Due to the pressure at Longridge caused by the launch of the Austin Allegro, the press demonstration cars were prepared at Abingdon, though the final shakedown testing, including running-in at MIRA, was carried out by the Redditch Press Garage. (Former Austin Morris PR man Ian Elliott was involved in the launch preparations and recalls that one of the press cars hit a pigeon at high speed during the run at MIRA:

Right: The press release on the V8 was issued in July, 1973...

Left: ...and this was how the car was advertised in national newspapers and motoring magazines.

'It came right through the windscreen; the interior of the car was wrecked!') Elliot further recollects: 'The national press drove the cars from Portman Square to a restaurant called Kinches, near Oxford. Unbeknown to them, their fuel consumption was checked, with a prize of a crate of beer for the best figure. I seem to remember that Judith Jackson was the winner, at 27mpg. Fuel consumption was, of course, a particularly topical subject at that time.'

Ian went on to borrow HOH 933L, the Harvest Gold V8 tested by *Motor* (and now owned by Syd Beer) for his honeymoon. 'My wife found the stiff rear springs a bit wearing, but I just kept enjoying the step-off!.'

Originally pencilled in for July the 18th, the launch finally took place on Wednesday, August the 15th. *Autocar* and *Motor* (which were subsequently to be merged) both appeared on Thursdays in those days and consequently the first published

Above: This graphic BL shot of the MGB GT V8 at speed (probably on the A420 near Tubney) shows off its classic Pininfarina lines to their best advantage. (Rover)

reactions to the car were those in the national newspapers. On the day of the launch, a full-page advertisement appeared in the *Daily Express*, whose correspondent David Benson, in an article entitled 'Borrowed Engine Peps Up New MG', welcomed the car as a logical amalgam of the classic MGB GT and Rover V8 power.

The following day, both *Autocar* and *Motor* profiled the V8, using skilled illustrators (Dick Ellis and Lawrence Watts respectively) to provide full cutaway views. *Autocar* stole a march on its rivals by publishing its road test in the same issue — its headline was 'MG Elegance, Rover Smoothness' — whereas *Motor*'s full test did not appear until two weeks later.

Both magazines were highly enthusiastic about the new V8, but were inevitably disappointed at the lack of development in the car's basic architecture. In common with other reporters, they found particular fault with the retention of the MGB GT's frameless side windows and prominent rain guttering channel and the consequent wind-noise when travelling at speed. In the smaller-engined car, this had been a reasonably tolerable drawback; in the faster and quieter-engined V8, it was perceived as a serious flaw.

Autocar was impressed by the V8's smooth delivery of performance: 'Never before has a sports car in this class been as flexible and forgiving and so easy to drive smoothly, but then never before has such a smooth engine been offered beneath the bonnet of an MG.' They were further impressed by the manner in which the car was able to deliver such

excellent performance and yet return remarkably economical fuel consumption: 'Compared with the last MGB GT that we tested two years ago, the V8 gave 23.4 mpg overall, compared with 23.7 mpg overall for the smaller-engined car... When the considerable difference in performance is taken into account, this is a quite outstanding achievement.' The magazine did, however, see potential problems in selling the car at such a high premium over its four-cylinder cousin, and in the face of such strong and mostly well-established opposition.

Motor's initial reactions were particularly favourable, even given what they themselves described as their normal cynicism. However, they went on to state: 'So appealing is the BV8 package that when the failings start to show themselves, there is a sense of disappointment.' Like *Autocar*, the testers were not impressed with the interior fittings or the ride of the car, and they were particularly scathing of the dashboard layout, which they contrasted with the excellent contemporary Triumph dashboards.

Performance merited four stars (out of a maximum of five) in *Motor*'s eyes because they felt that buyers were entitled to expect more from a 3.5-litre sports car in 1973 than the V8 delivered. Nevertheless, their car recorded the best 0-60mph time — 7.7 seconds — of any factory MGB GT V8 tested by an independent magazine. The factory figure was 8.25 seconds, and *Autocar*'s 8.6 seconds.

John Bolster, writing in the weekly *Autosport* on August the 16th, praised the V8's performance and criticised the wind noise. Interestingly, he was impressed by the lack of heat transfer into the cabin — a result, no doubt, of the extensive transmission tunnel cladding which anyone who has restored a V8 will be aware of! In a subsequent road test report, dated December the 27th, Bolster described the V8 succinctly as 'old wine in a new bottle', noting that 'to substitute a modern piece of light alloy engineering for an olde-tyme cast-iron lump must be progress'. The ex-Buick engine, dating as it did from the 1950s, was hardly the latest thing in engineering terms, but after the four-cylinder B-series engine it was certainly a major advance.

1973 marked the launch not only of the MGB GT V8 but also of a monthly magazine, *What Car?*, which was to become one of Britain's best-selling car journals. The first issue of *What Car?* appeared, in fact, at the 1973 Motor Show, where the V8 made its Earls Court debut, and featured a full road test on the V8. The car featured was a Bronze Yellow car, bearing the registration HOH902L which, according to the surviving records, should have been a Teal Blue car (chassis number GD2D1-119G)! The only Bronze car in the original press fleet was GD2D1-113G, which bore the registration number HOH 903L; this car is now in Holland. No doubt there was a mix-up with the registration numbers, not entirely unknown in press fleets.

After the initial excitement of the launch, relatively little was written about the V8, as most attention was centred on the facelift to the whole MG range for the autumn of the following year. A youthful Chris Goffey drove the first rubber-bumper V8 (now owned by Geoff and Jean Allen) as part of a large sports car group test for *Autocar*, published in the issue dated April the 5th, 1975. He and fellow-tester Andrew Shanks nominated the car as their favourite and found it refreshingly unusual for a powerful sports car of the era to be able to accommodate two small children in the back. Goffey summarised the MGB GT V8 as being 'my sort of car' and, many years later, proved it by buying an MGB V8 roadster for his own use.

Left: The impressive display on the MG stand at the October 1973 Earls Court Motor Show included this cutaway V8 engine, beautifully prepared by the Abingdon craftsmen. (Tom Studer)

Geoff Allen... Further Recollections

The Press Cars

The ten HOH...L registration-numbered press cars were very much in evidence around the middle months of 1973. Under normal circumstances, work would have been carried out on them at Austin Morris Publicity, but the imminent launch of the Austin Allegro led to their being transferred to Abingdon; they were built on the line between March the 6th and May the 10th, 1973, road-tested and rectified as normal production practice for all cars, then run on the road for 1200-1500 miles by MG staff members on evenings and weekends. Any faults which occurred were sorted out the following working day; among them were old favourites such as the steering pinion shaft fouling the offside exhaust manifold or the right-hand body side member (...a problem experienced by the RV8 development team almost 20 years later. — Author). Other problems included the oil cooler hoses fouling the right-hand side member — I recall that one car had to be trailed in as the pipe was cut through and all the engine oil was lost — and the fuel pipes jumping out of the two plastic clips below the heater box at the slightest provocation.

At the end of the running-in period, the cars were taken into Development and checked again before being taken by the Development staff to the MIRA test track for performance tests. On their return from MIRA, a report was compiled and the cars came back into Rectification for any outstanding work to be carried out.

During all this time there were only three of us working on the V8s, but as production increased, so did the number of workers; the factory was organised to allow anyone to work on any model, depending on demand. Generally speaking, the fitters either liked V8s or hated them, so by a process of natural selection they were worked through the shop by the same men over the production run. Over the 1973 Easter Bank Holiday, and for several days and overtime evenings afterwards, a number of shop rectification fitters worked on the ten press cars and two other cars (I think they were MMO 226L and MMO 229L) to remove the overdrive operation on third gear, due to problems with the gearbox in overdrive third. Most of the cars had a straightforward gearbox change, but on some we dismantled the gearbox and replaced the selector lever with the modified one which was eventually fitted to all V8s from gearbox number 1404 onwards. Also at this time we modified the oil gauge pipe take-off to pick up from the oil-pump base on these same 12 cars, after which they were re-tested and progressed into Paint Finishing, from where they would go out to the Main Agents.

In Production

To begin with, certain parts which were unique to the V8 were thin on the ground. One or two cars remained in the Rectification park for a period and were robbed of parts to complete the rectification of other cars. This situation resolved itself as production started to grow, and the cars began to accumulate in the Despatch car park.

In July, we returned from our annual holiday to find that most of the completed V8s had been delivered to the main agents in time for the launch in August. Figures have since shown that, of the 361 built on the line to that time, almost 300 were despatched during the last two weeks of July and 217 went out on Monday, July the 23rd.

During the following 'fuel crisis' months there was much talk of the possibilities of petrol rationing and of cuts in motorsport, together with the branding of any large-engined vehicle as a 'gas-guzzler': unsurprisingly, rumours of the V8 finishing were rife. Production did carry on, however, albeit rather erratically, with ten cars per day appearing to be the aim. Sometimes this figure was exceeded, but more often than not the reverse was the case, with no production at all during some weeks. For a while, V8s were only built during the last three days of the week.

During the run of chrome-bumpered cars, there were show cars for the annual Earls Court Motor Show, three for 1973 and two for 1974; and there was one for the 1973 Scottish Motor Show.

Production of chrome-bumpered cars, which were given the Works Classification 'Model 32', continued until October the 2nd, 1974, when GD2D1-1956G was mounted on the line. This was, in fact, about seven weeks after the first rubber-bumpered car, GD2D1-2101G. The last chrome-bumpered car to be despatched was GD2D1-1947G, on October the 21st, 1974.

In mid-August 1974 the first production rubber-bumpered car, which happened to be a V8, came into Rectification. Reactions were mixed, as they have been ever since. (I had no idea that 17 months later I would own this car myself, although I had for some time been on the firm's waiting-list for a used V8.) Rubber-bumpered V8s did not reach large production totals: only 733 were produced, compared with 1,858 chrome-bumpered cars. The first 531 retained the old 'Model 32' classification. The last 202, classified 'Model 3004', ran from September the 12th, 1975 (which saw the mounting of GD2D1-2701G, the show model for that year), until July the 13th, 1976, when GD2D1-2903G was mounted.

It was announced during the final year of V8 production that any staff member applying for an MGB GT 'Management Car Plan' (MCP) car would be issued with a V8 rather than the 1.8-litre four, which would explain why 27 of the last 202 V8s were MCP cars. The V8 story came to an end on October the 13th, 1976, when GD2D1-2902G left the factory. The last two cars, which included some of the features of the 1977 model year facelifted MGB range, were said to have been built in the hope of persuading British Leyland to sanction a continuation of V8 production. If so, it was sadly to no avail.

As a postscript, during my postponed holiday in Torquay in October 1976, we stopped to put some petrol in our Teal Blue MGB GT V8 and the petrol pump attendant (remember them?) told us, 'We have a picture of a car like this on our calendar'. I replied that it probably *was* our car, and when he produced the calendar we found that this was indeed the case. The attendant, who had not even known that the V8 existed, asked to see under the bonnet and was further surprised to learn that almost

2,600 V8s had been built. He had thought that the picture on the calendar was of an MGB with special wheels fitted, and as the photo had been taken from the offside front, with no V8 badge visible, I could understand why. As soon as we were home again, I fitted a V8 badge to the front of the car…

Preparation of Show Cars at Abingdon

The show car bodies which arrived at Abingdon from the Pressed Steel works at Swindon had always been assembled with extra care. All the seams in the engine compartment, spare wheel compartment, doors, tailgate, bonnet and door-shut areas had been filled; all the paint-work, including engine and spare wheel compartments, was of a very high standard; and the same attention had been paid to the interior trim.

In the Rectification and Paint Finishing shops at Abingdon, in 'B' Block, the rocker covers were removed and the unpainted ribs were polished before being carefully masked up and painted black. The inlet adaptors were repainted with a high-quality heatproof black paint and the carburettor dashpots were buffed and refitted. On some of the cars, we removed the inlet manifolds and painted them and the main body of the engine Steel Dust Grey. The engine compartment components (heater boxes, washer brackets, pedal boxes, expansion tank, radiator etc) were stripped and repainted in cellulose before being taken to the line for fitting.

Brake, clutch. fuel and oil pipes were checked for position and shape, and wiring was re-taped and positioned for neat appearance. Parts such as door catches and striker plates, radiator and expansion tank caps, hose clips, engine mounting brackets, air filter clips and bolts, heater box clips and air intake shrouds were chromium-plated at the old Morris Radiators factory in Bainton Road, Oxford. At least one show car had a plated metal vacuum pipe fitted. Usually Inspection sorted all through the fascias and bumpers to find the best ones available (this did not stop us having to check them again if a better one turned up later), the bodies were rechecked, the doors, bonnet and tailgate were refitted and the trim was given extra attention, especially such flimsy items as the cardboard fillets to the windscreen pillars and rear header rails. Dummy radios consisting of only case, dial and knobs were fitted, as were dummy batteries, without plates or acid; no oil, water, hydraulic fluid or fuel was inserted. The seat-back release lever knobs were stuck on with Araldite (at an earlier Show, someone had cut his hand on the lever after the knob had been stolen), and so were the gear lever knobs. Number plates bearing the legend 'MGBGTV8', with the BL logo to the right-hand side, were attached and painted the same colour as the bodywork.

Inside the cars, at both sides on the cantrails above the doors and B posts, 18-inch fluorescent tubes were fitted, with the wiring passing down through the rear quarter panels into the spare wheel compartment, where the operating gear was mounted. The mains power cable passed out through one of the blanking grommet holes in the floor. One car — from memory, the Citron V8 displayed at the 1973 Earls Court Show — also had a strip light fitted across the front, somewhere around the radiator area.

On the rubber-bumper cars, the inside of the engine compartment was painted matt black, including the front of the radiator diaphragms. (One year, the top rails of the front bumpers were packed inside with plastic filler to prevent children from pulling the plastic bumper off the frame. This was not done again due to the Trades Descriptions Act, although a disclaimer was put on the cars pointing out that they were built to Show standards.) Finally the cars went into Paint Finishing where they were re-checked yet again and anything which had been overlooked was rectified. One of the very last tasks was to disconnect the bonnet release cables and fit a hidden pull, to prevent the bonnet being opened when no attendant was near.

On the cars' return from the show, seats, floormats and any other damaged parts were changed, the strip lights were removed and new cantrail covers fitted; all liquids were added, and proper batteries were installed. Either radio blanks or new radios were fitted, and all the bright parts and number plates were removed and stored for the next year. The cars then went back into Paint Finishing again and from there to the dealers.

All this work was carried out by a small group of six of us in Rectification and Paint Finishing, over the September holiday period and during weekends and evenings during the following fortnight or so. It was always a great relief to see the cars depart to Earls Court. As long as they remained in the factory, someone would inevitably point out some minor blemish, and out would come the tools again that evening. Sometimes this would mean a trip over to 'A' Block with a torch to search an unfamiliar pro-duction line in the dark for a part fitted on heaven knows what stage of the line during assembly. (Don't kid yourself, for example, that the fuel filler cap was fitted anywhere near the stage at which the fuel tank was fitted; it was not even on the same floor!) Still, it did earn me a week's holiday when all the others were working, so I couldn't complain…

Left: *The MGB GT V8 tested by Autocar was recently restored to its full glory by V8 Register member Steve Cox, who bought the car unaware of its history until he came across a copy of the magazine by chance. (David Knowles)*

Production Changes

Various running changes took place during the early stages of MGB GT V8 production, including improvements to the oil gauge and take off, modifications to the gearbox of some early cars (which had slipped through with overdrive on third gear as well as top) and minor changes in trim materials consistent with those in the remainder of the MGB range. *(See appendices for full details.)*

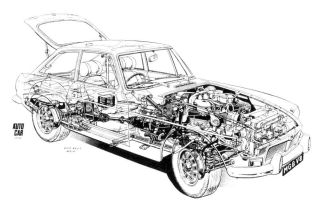

Above and Below: Autocar *and* Motor *both featured fine cutaways of the V8 in their coverage of its arrival.* *(Autocar & Motor)*

The major market for sports cars — and one that was of course vitally important to British Leyland with their MG, Triumph and Jaguar ranges — was the United States. In the wake of the Clean Air Act of 1968, and the Ralph Nader-inspired onslaught on primary vehicle safety, any manufacturer selling cars in the USA had to carry out a thorough product overhaul in order to comply with the new statutory legislation. Bureaucracy ran riot, the certification papers for each model were many inches thick, and consequently the effort required to ensure that cars could remain on sale became enormously costly.

From the autumn of 1973, for the 1974 model year, cars sold in the USA had to comply with impact legislation which meant that the vehicle should be able to survive a front or rear end impact of up to 5mph with minimal damage; this resulted, in the case of the MG Midget, MGB, Triumph Spitfire, Triumph TR6 and Jaguar E-type, in large and rather ugly reinforced rubber over-riders, which were designed to pass any impact loads back to the body structure. One small but noticeable effect of this was that the rear number plate illumination lamps, which had hitherto been mounted on the inboard faces of the rear over-riders, were of necessity moved to new locations on the bumper itself; this is why later chrome-bumper MGB GT V8s (and all MGBs of the same period, of course) may usually be identified by the location of the rear number plate lamps. 'Usually' because, in typical Abingdon fashion, a box of 50 or more of the original specification bumpers was discovered under a bench one day, and these were duly fitted to UK market cars going down the line!

For the 1975 model year, the requirements called for no impact damage whatsoever. This resulted in further changes, the most obvious of which was the adoption across the MG sports car range of the massive full-width black bumpers. Jim O'Neill, responsible for engineering the rubber bumpers (styled by Harris Mann), recalls the task as one of the most difficult of his entire working life: 'We were faced with the stark fact that unless we conformed with the latest USA regulations, the end of MG production would be imminent. The regulations called for a vehicle to be able to sustain an impact of 5mph with no damage whatsoever — even to the extent of a cracked lens. Many months were spent trying to develop a suitable bumper system — hydraulics, leaf springs and canvas-reinforced rubber were tried, but all proved unacceptable. It soon became apparent that a polyurethane bumper, constructed in such a way as to absorb an impact progressively, was our only hope; and even this was proving difficult at the stipulated -40°. I visited the authorities in Washington for a clarification or easing of their requirements but to no avail — although since then, of course, the US authorities have considerably relaxed the relevant legislation.

'The MG bumper design which eventually emerged was patented by British Leyland and allowed us another five years' production. I must also acknowledge the assistance given to

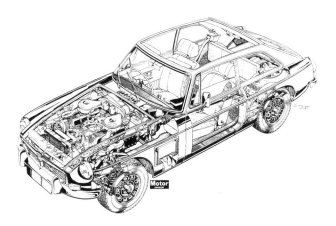

us by Marley Foam Ltd, who went on to manufacture the production bumpers, and by Davidson's in the USA, who helped with the low-temperature testing.'

O'Neill is forthright about the appearance of these bumpers, which aroused so much controversy: 'To conform with the regulations, we needed a bumper depth of six inches. Imagine what this looked like when applied to a small car!

'By styling the bumper material up and around the grille, a more acceptable shape was arrived at, disguising the massive steel armature beneath.

'I worked very closely with Harris Mann on the styling aspects, and in spite of all the criticism I still feel it was a very creditable effort. Yes, there *were* people at MG who thought that the rubber bumpers were atrocities, especially with the increase in weight they imposed. Nevertheless *I* liked them, and I know what type of MGB I would prefer to be driving if I were to be involved in an accident!'

Whereas the original MGB GT V8 had been assigned a separate Project Code, ADO75 (the MGB, you will recall, had been ADO23), the whole MGB range for 1975 onwards was allocated a new code of ADO76, since the changes needed were the most extensive (and expensive) in the history of the MGB family. It has already been described how tentative plans to export the MBG GT V8 to North America were abandoned, but nevertheless the demands of that market had an overwhelming effect on each and every MG sports car, since the vast majority were exported there — and most of them went to California, the state with the toughest legislation of all. (Cars sold outside California were known as '49 State' cars, since they were prohibited from being sold there).

Consequently, although the EEC- and home-market legislators had no requirement at that stage for onerous crash certification of the type being adopted in the USA, simple economics dictated that the structure of all of the cars should be modified to suit North American requirements. Thus, the large black bumpers were adopted across the entire MG range.

In addition to the impact legislation, there were related requirements which dictated the height of the bumpers — presumably in a rather feeble attempt by the authorities to standardise bumper height. MG found that they had to raise the suspension of the standard MGB by an almost unbelievable 1.5 inches in order to comply with this ruling, ruining at one fell swoop the MGB's previously well-balanced handling. As Don Hayter explained: 'The notorious 'bumper standard' dictated a test with a pendulum at heights between 16 inches and 20 inches, which gave an impact load line well above the MGB chassis members. This height was derived from the average height of the comparatively big American cars of the period. We therefore raised the body datum relative to the suspension mounting points by one inch and the other half-inch was in the suspension and springs themselves.'

Understandably, there was anguish among British MG enthusiasts, who were horrified that the MGB, whose power output had been progressively falling anyway, was saddled with these enormous and extremely heavy bumpers which added over a hundred pounds to its weight; nor did they appreciate the raised suspension. The combination of these factors produced a car which handled and performed more poorly than its predecessor and, in many people's opinion, looked ugly into the bargain. These people were in most cases unaware of the extensive re-engineering of the basic body structure which had been necessary to accommodate these new bumpers, at the front in particular. Such were the alterations behind the bumpers that anyone wishing neatly to convert to chrome bumpers would find the task a good deal more complex than anticipated.

Public opinion often tends to change over the years, and the rubber-bumper MGB models nowadays have loyal and

How US Legislation Nearly Killed

The Open Sports Car

Almost everyone who is old enough remembers the dramatic effect of US Government legislation on the domestic car market during the early 1970s, though perhaps not all appreciate how close the world came to losing the open sports car altogether. The real threat to its survival came in the winter of 1971-72 with the publication of Federal Motor Vehicle Safety Standard 208, relating to the protection of vehicle occupants in the event of a collision. The most important aspect of this legislation as far as open cars were concerned was the introduction of a new roll-over test: vehicles would be tested by rolling from a platform moving at 30mph, and it was stipulated in MVSS 208 that all the occupants of the vehicle would have to remain wholly within it. It was a fairly difficult task to guarantee this even in a vehicle with a roof; in an open car it was virtually impossible, yet the National Highway Traffic Safety Administration (NHTSA) was adamant that there could be no allowances made for such vehicles. The ultimate goal of MVSS 208 appeared to be the ability to retain occupants within the vehicle without the need for any conscious effort on their part. Seat-belts, in other words, were not the answer; only airbags would do.

Some firms began to explore the possibility of 'targa tops', whilst many others — particularly the 'big three' domestic manufacturers — decided to give up the open-car market altogether and to fight the legislation where it affected the rest of their output. Chrysler mounted a major legal onslaught against MVSS 208 in order to avoid the imposition of airbags — but, at the same time, pursued the case for the open convertible in a suit against the Department of Transportation. The results of Chrysler's action — which was largely successful — were not only a delay in the imposition of airbags without an executive-branch review, but also a conclusion that the 1970 Highway Safety Act did not empower the NHTSA effectively to eliminate any existing types of car — specifically open-top vehicles. The legal interpretation was that 'people knowingly accept certain risks when they choose this type of machinery over what may well be a safer automobile.'

Convertibles still had to provide adequate safety provision — including lap belts, the ability to meet the requirements of a windscreen pillar crush test, and the normal horizontal impact requirements common to all vehicles — but manufacturers were saved the unenviable task of trying to provide an airbag system to contain unrestrained occupants in a car with no roof. Yet, even so, the NHTSA was far from defeated: in the ten months between the issuing of MVSS 208 and the outcome of the Chrysler court case in November 1972, a number of convertibles in the planning stage had been consigned to the scrapheap, with budgets redirected to the ever-growing mountain of other new legislation. Among the victims of this period of indecision were the Triumph TR7 and the Jaguar XJ-S, both due to be launched within the following two years — and, without doubt, any plans for an open MGB V8 roadster would also have been abandoned. All three of these cars emerged solely as coupés, with the extensively re-engineered open-top derivatives of the TR7 and XJ-S not arriving until much later. Long-serving open-top cars, such as the four-cylinder MGB, the Midget, the Spitfire, the TR6, the Jaguar E-type and the Alfa Romeo Spyder were left unscathed; but for those few months in 1972, it really did seem as though the death-knell of the open-top sports car had been sounded.

dedicated followers, who are keen to point out the way in which the styling of the new RV8 bumpers appears to have evolved from that of the late MGB GT V8. The author can further testify to the strength of the bumper units, which remained undamaged on his own MGB GT despite a number of minor confrontations with lesser vehicles!

Don Hayter points out that 'the actual cornering ability of the car was hardly affected — it just felt a lot worse!' Only after the V8 had been discontinued would rear anti-roll bars be fitted to the MGB, in an attempt to cure the excessive rolls caused by the raised suspension, but even then the improvements made were not sufficient to rectify the problem completely.

In line with this rubber-bumper MGB facelift, the GT V8, which by now was being produced at a trickle in proportion to mainstream MGB and GT production, was modified in similar manner. However, the MGB GT V8 already had a higher suspension than the MGB, so it was not thought necessary to raise it any further. Many more parts were now common to the four-cylinder and V8 cars, including much of the engine bay panelwork which had hitherto remained exclusive to the V8; but the small-engined cars retained their original radiator mountings and thus still differed slightly from their bigger-engined brothers.

Below: Two former press V8s pictured at a recent V8 Register gathering. In the foreground is the ex-Autocar test car owned by Steve Cox. HOH 901L, behind it, was tested by Car magazine and is now owned by Mike Dunlop. (David Knowles)

Left: A press V8 cornering at speed. According to the surviving records, HOH 905L should have been a Glacier White car, which suggests that registration numbers might have been allocated on a fairly flexible basis. (Tom Studer)

Left: This former factory development car, chassis number ADO 75/413, is now proudly owned by Graham Smith of Frome, Somerset, whose father used to work for MG at Abingdon. Unusually, the factory development log book for the car also survives and is in Graham Smith's keeping. (Graham Smith)

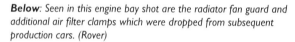

Below: Seen in this engine bay shot are the radiator fan guard and additional air filter clamps which were dropped from subsequent production cars. (Rover)

Right: Geoff Allen at the wheel of 'Teal Blue 2101', on Chain Hill, near Wantage, in February 1992. (Popular Classics)

The End Of The Road

There have been many explanations put forward for why the MGB GT V8 foundered, and doubtless each contains its own germ of truth. It has often been argued, for example, that the sequence of events giving rise to the car, largely in response to a private enterprise conversion, showed that in the eyes of the mandarins at BL the V8 was little more than an aberration, a temporary sop to MG and the dealer network who would soon, they presumably believed, be clamouring for the new Triumph sports cars waiting in the wings.

For all the enthusiasm it generated, the V8 was not the all-new sports car which Abingdon wanted. We saw in Chapter One that the MG designers had built a prototype replacement for the MGB in 1968 — coded EX-234 — only to see that project canned. They had put a great deal of engineering work into the mid-engined AD021 proposal, to

the extent of trying out the proposed Maxi 1750 running gear in a specially converted MGB GT bodyshell; but that too had been cancelled, in favour of the more conventional Triumph 'Bullet' sports car (which emerged, in 1975, as the TR7).

For those willing to see it, the MG factory had clearly been hanging on by the skin of its teeth — an intolerable situation, bearing in mind its importance to the parent company as the producer of some its more significant exports and a major dollar earner. Nor was this state of affairs of merely recent origin. As Geoff Allen recalls: 'I was told shortly after I had joined that I had made a mistake; I was told that we would soon all be out of work as the factory would be closed — and that was in 1954!' The powers-that-be were largely guilty of wasting enormous amounts of money on ultimately abortive or unsuccessful projects, whilst Abingdon survived with some autonomy but on a shoestring. By the time Leyland came on the scene, much of the damage had already been done.

Right: The interior of the MGB GT V8 was similar to the contemporary MGB GT, with the addition of standard head restraints (which became an option for the smaller-engined car). The larger steering column cowl, and the smaller instrument nacelle with the 80mm speedometer and tachometer, can be seen in this shot. (Rover)

Left: This is an early rubber-bumper MGB GT V8 from 1974/5, as evidenced by the body-coloured front valance, but more particularly by the lack of the small black and chrome 'BGT' trim badge at the top of the C-Pillar. (Rover)

British Leyland pumped a reputed £96 million into the Triumph TR7, including the building of a completely new factory at Speke, yet seemed reluctant to offer MG more than the merest pittance. In the words of a former MG employee: 'Stokes didn't like us because we didn't have a moving line at Abingdon'.

As has been shown, the MGC had seriously undermined MG's reputation. Certainly it had lent support to those who argued that new sports car development should be centred on Canley or Longbridge — conveniently ignoring the fact that MG consistently outsold their rivals. Further, MG's relatively small development team, coupled with their dependence upon the North American market, meant that the increasingly tough US automotive legislation of the period kept Abingdon fully stretched just ensuring that their cars continued to meet emissions and strength requirements and remain on sale. Around the time of the launch of the V8, MG were working on the changes necessary to keep the Midget available in North America — and later, of course, on the 1974 and 1975 impact requirements on all models — so that the V8 project, though a source of pride at the factory, was certainly not the greatest priority.

Once the decision to produce the V8 had been made, it was restricted to a GT version; this was not because the open version was insufficiently strong, as has so often been reported, but primarily because, on the one hand, MG believed that they could sell as many GTs as they could get engines, and, on the other hand, because it was felt that a high-powered car should be a coupé rather than a soft top, particularly once it was decided to aim the car at performance coupé rivals. There were also some doubts about the future of *any* open-top sports car in the all-important North American market (see sidebar), which was the principal reason why the TR7 first appeared as a hard top coupé; but as soon as it was decided not to export the V8, this argument became irrelevant.

According to Ian Elliott, the MGB GT V8 was on and off a number of times in 1972, particularly once the decision not to

export the car had been made, but as much as anything else there was the desire to challenge the might of Ford's three-litre Capri with Austin Morris' own 'wild car'. But here, as is explained later, the element of price became even more significant.

J. Bruce McWilliams was keen to see the V8 exported to the USA, in whatever form, but his pleas fell on deaf ears. As already described, some development work was done on 'cleaning up' the engine, including the installation of air pumps and other anti-smog equipment, and of course the low-lead specification of the engine was ideally suited to unleaded petrol use. But British Leyland refused to sanction the necessary expenditure to certify the V8 engine, despite (because of?) the fact that it was already planned at that stage for introduction in the Triumph TR8 by around 1977, just four years after the MGB GT V8 was launched.

The limited number of engines available to MG, contributing to the V8 being launched only as a GT, was seen by the MG people as being largely a political move by those in power at Longbridge, and it is fair to say that given a freer hand MG could have adopted the later Rover SD1 engine (an early prototype of which, ironically, was tested in an MGB GT V8, now owned by Graham Smith) and the V8 could have been made more of a success.

In later years, research by noted author Graham Robson suggested that Rover's Solihull engine facility could have produced many more V8 engines than were actually being used. In his book *The Mighty MGs*, Robson stated that in 1973 Range Rovers were being built at a rate of about 150 cars a week, and V8-engined Rover saloons were being turned out at around 200 a week. Morgan soaked up a mere five or so units per week, and so with MG's 50 a week the total came to a weekly 400 V8 engines — which, as Robson pointed out, Rover could easily have exceeded if the appropriate decisions had been made.

At no time, Robson estimated, did MG take more than 10 percent of Rover V8 engine production, and the fall in sales of the Rover P6 during the 1973-4 energy crisis meant that MG should have been able to absorb a larger proportion of V8 engine production. It was true that the all-new Rover SD1 would use a large number of (improved) engines, but this car did not enter production until three years after the MGB GT V8 was launched.

In correspondence with the author, David Wall, who was Rover's Chief Engine Designer of the period, recalled that Solihull were not in fact geared up to produce enough engines: 'It was our intention to up production to over two thousand V8's per week, but this was forestalled by the fuel crisis.' However, Wall agrees with Robson's prognosis that output could have been raised: 'At one stage, the V8 cylinder block transfer machining was duplicated'. He also doubts that General Motors had any say in the uses to which British Leyland put the V8 engine: 'GM were always mildly amused that anyone should wish to buy the rights to an outdated (to them) engine of which they had already produced three-quarters of a million examples!'

By the time the MG V8 came on the scene, the P6B 3500 saloon had a limited life and the new SD1 was still on the horizon, and this may at least partly explain why a higher-performance engine was not adopted.

Unfortunately the whole scenario of what was happening to MG *vis-a-vis* Triumph inevitably contributed to the downfall of the V8: at the end of 1974, after a few North American specification black-bumper 1798cc MGB GTs had been built, it was decided to withdraw the GT from the US market, despite howls of protest from the importers, ostensibly because the car, due largely to its greater weight, could no longer meet the emissions requirements. Attempts by Don Hayter and others to lighten the car (including the consideration of reintroducing the alloy bonnet which British Leyland had dropped in 1970) were thrown out on cost grounds, and the withdrawal of the North American specification GT body-shell almost certainly dealt the export potential of the V8 its death-blow.

The Jubilee MGB GT V8

The Golden Jubilee of the MG Car Company occurred in 1974, but was not celebrated by British Leyland until the following year. To mark the occasion, it was decided to build 750 MGB GTs in a special colour scheme of British Racing Green with gold side flashes, appropriate Jubilee insignia and V8-style Dunlop wheels which had gold rims and centre casting 'highlights' instead of the normal V8's bright chrome and polished alloy.

At the end of the production run, it transpired that there were sufficient materials left over to produce one further car. (In the final event, 752 were built, but that is another story!) This car was offered to David Haddon, Managing Director of the British School of Motoring. Haddon said that he would like it built as a V8 version and Abingdon duly complied; BSM had, after all, been extremely good customers of British Leyland. Commissioned on June the 18th, 1975, and assigned the V8 chassis number GD2D1-2605G, the car left the factory just one week later. It was registered as 1 BSM, though this was later changed to MGB 5 when the BSM plate was transferred to another vehicle.

Haddon, who nowadays runs his own consultancy business, recalls his Jubilee V8 with affection, describing it as 'a bloody beast of a car'. It remained in his possession for a year — during which it helped promote the BSM 'HPC' high-performance driving course — and has subsequently seen several changes of ownership. Recently restored, it is now in the hands of an anonymous owner in the UK.

Below: Rear view of the early rubber-bumper V8, with a made-up registration number. Note the use of chrome-plated number plate lights; these were not changed to black plastic on the MGB until the V8 ceased production. (Rover)

Cynics are also keen to point out that the withdrawal of the GT (which had always been a steady seller in all markets) preceded the introduction of the Triumph TR7 which was, of course, launched as a fixed-head car only... Ironically, as Wilson McComb related in his seminal MG history, *MG By McComb*: 'In America, there was an extraordinary *volte-face* as a demand began to grow for the evergreen MGB GT to be brought back as a replacement for the TR7, and Triumph embarked upon redesigning their new model as an open car to compete more effectively with the old MGB.' Of course there was by then too much investment in the Triumph TR7 and the prospect of too much egg on the corporate face, so the GT remained obstinately a home-market only car, where its sales held up remarkably well, particularly as a fashionable 'sports hatchback' for well-heeled young ladies.

And, of course, there is the economic perspective. 1973 was a year in which price rises were becoming a regular part of everyday life and the word 'inflation' part of the common vocabulary — a scenario which could only promote caution amongst potential buyers. Nor were matters helped by the Arab-Israeli war, which led to the perception of large-engined sports cars as uneconomic and unfashionable anachronisms.

When launched in August, the V8 cost (including car tax and VAT) £2,293.96; by the end of its first year, the price had climbed by some 22 percent to £2,795.13; and by the autumn of 1975 it had risen to £3,371.94 — almost half as much again as the price on launch.

Ford's three-litre Capri, with its torquey Essex V6 engine, was a potent if unsophisticated car, available with a wide variety of trim options and offering four proper seats in a sleek coupé body. When MG launched their V8, the Capri could be bought for just £1,651, an advantage which in today's terms would equate to some five or six thousand pounds. The MG's pedigree was undeniable and the power under its bonnet would have made its own appeal, but neither of these elements would have compensated for the substantial price difference.

By comparison with the other cars considered its major rivals, the V8's launch price was not unreasonable. Unfortunately, the comparison made by the buying public was usually with the four-cylinder MGB, where the difference was in most people's view extremely difficult to justify.

The last word on the subject may be left to John Thornley: 'The MGB GT V8 retained the weight, balance and behavioural characteristics of the MGB with power roughly equivalent to that of the MGC. It was a very, very good motor car, so good in fact that it aroused a deal of jealousy among competing factions within BL. Production was constantly interrupted by engine shortages and some of the decisions as to where, or more particularly where not, it should be marketed could not be explained in normal terms.'

Top: One of the very few MG V8s to be found in America, this one was purchased by Oklahoman Don Peery during a trip to England in 1985. The only obvious exterior change is the addition of side marker lights to meet US requirements. Doors are also American, with internal side impact beams. (Don Peery)

Left: The first and last MGB GT V8s were brought together for the first and perhaps only time in the V8 Register's marquee at the MG Car Club Silverstone weekend in May 1992. (Thanks to Eric Prasse and British Motor Heritage.) (David Knowles)

Right: The Costello MGB V8's most distinctive features were the prominent bonnet bulge (confined to early cars, such as this 1972 example) and the specially-fabricated matt black 'egg-box' grille. The wheels on this car are those of the subsequent factory V8. (Mark Vine)

Below: The engine bay of Mark Vine's Costello V8, showing the standard Rover P6 V8 power unit with the inclined SU carburettors mounted in the vee of the engine. (Mark Vine)

Below right: The rear of original Costello V8s featured this distinctive 'V Eight Costello' badge which was styled to blend in with the contemporary MGB GT badges. (Autocar)

Below: Although preceded by at least one development car, this is generally accepted as the first pre-production prototype MGB GT V8. It bears the chassis number GD2D1-99G and is known colloquially as 'Flame 99'. Now owned by Robin Dodson, it was retained by the factory for a number of years after the V8 had been launched and shows signs of having been used for development purposes. (Robin Dodson)

Left: Owned by Dutchman Bas Geritts, this is the second production V8 and also one of the trio sent to North America in 1972. It was later sold to Brian Field and had quite a successful competition career before ending up in Geritts' care. Note the US-specification side marker lights on the wings. (Bas Geritts)

Right: The beautifully trimmed interior of Bas Geritts' car is fitted with non-original but very smart blue leather seats, headlining and sun visors. The lhd dashboard is the same as that of the contemporary North American specification four-cylinder MGB. (Bas Geritts)

Below: Tom Studer of Switzerland owns another of the early lhd production V8s, in this case GD2D2-DUD-109G. As can be seen from this photograph, he does not believe in keeping the car under wraps! (Tom Studer/Motorsport-Fotos)

Below: Roger Righini's immaculate Teal Blue lhd car, pictured at home in Lausanne, Switzerland. The car had covered 76,000 miles by late 1993, and still has the original engine (numbered 49000007). Note the Italian market all-white front indicator lenses fitted to this car. (Roger Righini)

Right: Like Bas Geritts, Roger Righini has retrimmed the interior in leather (Autumn Leaf in place of the original Ochre). The gauges in the centre console are later additions. (David Knowles)

Below right: Launched at the 1973 Earls Court Motorshow, the monthly magazine What Car? tested a Bronze V8 in its very first issue. There is some confusion in the official factory records — this car should, it seems, have been HOH 903L. (What Car?)

Below: Perhaps a clue as to why there appears to have been a mix-up with the registration number of the car which What Car? tested is evident in this factory photograph of an early V8: there is no record of a car which actually bore the registration number YWL 667L, so this is almost certainly the same car, but with a different number. (Rover)

Above: The centrepiece of the MG stand at the 1973 Motor Show was this dramatically elevated Citron-coloured car (GD2D1-798G) which was displayed over a sectioned V8 engine. Note the very high standard of preparation of the underbody, which was specially painted black (cars were normally body colour underneath). The Citroen GS in the background was also making its UK Show debut. (Rover)

Above: Much of the early promotional literature for the V8 featured this Damask Red example — almost certainly GD2D1-103G — pictured here against a crimson studio back-drop for, among other things, the V8 sales leaflet. Number-plate is false. (Ian Elliott)

Left: The extra clips on the air-cleaners and the radiator fan guard — superfluous since the twin electric fans are mounted ahead of the radiator — identify this as an early V8. The oil-gauge take-off from the remote oil filter was modified after about 1,100 cars had been built. (Rover)

52

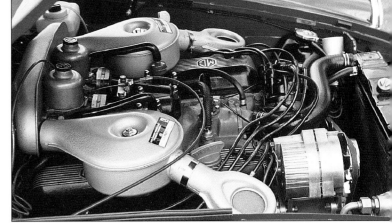

Right: By way of comparison with the early production car, this is the engine bay of the author's 1974 MGB GT V8, GD2D1- 1215G. Additional clips have been deleted from the air cleaner housings and there is no integral radiator fan guard. The brass radiator plug is a non-original but desirable replacement for the plastic original. (David Knowles)

Right: The interior of the original MGB GT V8 differed from the contemporary MGB GT in that the main instrumentation (speedometer and tachometer) was smaller in size and fitted in a shallower cowl to accommodate the collapsible steering column. This picture shows the V8's 'black crackle' finish to good effect. (Ian Elliott)

Below: YWL 921L was a Glacier White car which featured in British Leyland press releases at the time of the launch. This rare colour shot was taken at Blenheim Palace. (Rover)

53

Above: With the adoption of rubber bumpers in late 1974, the V8 began to look even less distinguishable from the four-cylinder 'B. This photograph was taken for the 1975 brochure; note the body-coloured front valance, twin bumper-mounted towing eyes and absence of a C-pillar GT trim flash — all features which were altered for the final 1976 model year. (Ian Elliott)

Left: Pictured for the 1973 MG model range brochure. the V8 is seen here alongside the contemporary 1798cc four-cylinder car. Model 'Saskia' (Pat Parkes) appeared in a number of British Leyland photographs of the period. (Ian Elliott)

Left: The October 1974 MGB GT & V8 brochure featured this Glacier White V8 on its cover. Note the chrome-finished badges and the red background to the front MG badge. Both MG and V8 badges were changed to a gold finish for 1975, with the background to the MG badges painted black.

Below: Former MG Development Department employee Bob Neville had raced the ex-Roger Enever MG Midget with success for a number of years. In May 1973 he made the decision to prepare a racing V8 and first appeared in the MGCC races in 1975. The car is seen here at Silverstone in May 1976, during pre-qualifying practice for its debut in the World Sportscar Championship. It went on to take an impressive eighth place and to make history as the only MG V8 (and the last Abingdon MG) to score World Championship points. (Bob Neville)

Above: The Stratstone-sponsored MGB GT V8 on its way to sixteenth place at Brands Hatch in September 1977. (Tom Studer)

Right: Brian Field began rallying his V8 in 1974 and has been enjoying himself ever since. Here he is pictured with his co-driver (who rejoices in the nickname 'Mad Mal') on the Epynt 'Harry Flatters' stage in 1990. The car finished first in the Historic category and 19th overall. (Brian Field)

Below left: Field's second left-hand-drive MGB GT V8 was this ex-US assessment car, which he sold to Peter Rushforth in 1976. Rushforth continued to campaign the car, together with Michael Pearson-Kirk, and it is seen here in the 1977 International Welsh Rally. (Foster & Skeffington)

Below right: Brian Field's Harvest Gold MGB GT V8 during the same event. (Foster & Skeffington)

Above: A powerful line-up of leading V8 contenders at Brands Hatch in the 1980 MG Car Club BCV8 Championship. Rod Longton leads, closely followed by Chris O'Neil, Steve Williams, Richard Horne, Keith Guerrier and Bill Beadnell. (Photo Steve Jones, courtesy Rod Longton)

Left: Rod Longton, a retired GP, currently races this car. It was bought from fellow BCV8 Championship competitor Bob Slessor as a half-finished V8 project and Longton initially ran it as a 1950cc four-cylinder car. With the arrival of the RV8 and the launch of the new Class C MGB V8s, the car has reverted to V8 status. Power is from a 3.9-litre limited-tune engine, TVR bell-housing and Sierra Cosworth gearbox. It is seen here dicing with Warwick Banks at Snetterton in 1993. (Photo Steve Jones, courtesy Rod Longton)

Below: One of the first full-race MGB GT V8s to appear after the Bob Neville/Malcolm Beer car was Colin Pearcy's. Pearcy raced the car for a number of years before selling it to Keith Guerrier in 1987. It is seen here at Silverstone in 1992, in the hands of MG Midget champion Graeme Adams who acquired it in 1991. (Brian Halford)

Right: The launch of the Heritage MGB bodyshells in 1987 made it possible to contemplate the idea of a V8-engined MGB roadster, something which the Abingdon factory never produced. This car was built by proud owner Brian Galipeau, seen here at speed with his wife. Note the subtle lack of V8 badging! (Classic & Sportcar).

Right: Ken Costello built this immaculately detailed MGB GT V8 in 1991 for a well-known television personality. The car features a 4.2-litre Rover V8 engine with low-profile Costello fuel injection (eliminating the need for a bonnet bulge), Costello's own unique five-speed gearbox and anti-lock braking. (David Reeves, Central TV)

Above right: The beautifully finished engine bay of the 1991 Costello MGB GT V8. Note the nice detailing of the injection plenum chamber cover, complete with 'Costello' logo. (David Reeves, Central TV)

Below: One of a number of development 'hacks', this black car was built using a Heritage bodyshell, with the only real clue to its identity being the RV8-style alloy wheels, flared rear wheel arches and bonnet bulge. Car magazine was fortunate in being invited by Rover to try the car ahead of the availability of any full production examples. The testers were favourably impressed and the car, with an MGB hard top, is seen here at speed. (Car)

Left: This concept drawing for the RV8 shows the development of the body shape of the car from its MGB roots. Note the slight flare to the wheel arches, the square-shaped bonnet bulge and rubber bumper-style front end. (Rover)

Left: Another styling proposal shows the car without a bonnet bulge (which is technically feasible but would have required modifications to the shape of the Land Rover-designed plenum chamber) and differently detailed wing flaring. The nose of this car could give a clue to the possible shape of a future all-new MG sports car. (Rover)

Below: A finished but unpainted RV8 bodyshell waiting to leave the Faringdon-based British Motor Heritage bodyshell production facility. Smaller picture shows the interior of the Heritage facility with bodyshells in preparation. (Autocar & Motor)

Above: The team behind the RV8 manufacturing facility at Cowley, pictured with the first production car (now in the Heritage Museum in Gaydon). Immediately behind the celebratory notice is Production Manager Cliff Law, whilst behind him is Graham Irvine, the project's Director. On the other side of the car is Roy Belcher, who worked at Abingdon from 1954 to 1980 and is now delightedly part of the MG story once more. (Rover)

MG RV8
VIN : 000251
FIRST PRODUCTION
VEHICLE COMPLETES ASSEMBLY
APRIL 1993

Right: Cliff Law stands proudly amid a trio of completed RV8s at the Cowley production facility. These cars are about to go out on test, prior to final valeting and delivery. (David Knowles)

Below: This view shows almost the whole of the main production line at Cowley, the car in the foreground being virtually complete. (David Knowles)

59

Left: The RV8 bodies are carried on adapted motorised slings which support the shells until the suspension units have been installed. *(David Knowles)*

Left: This official photograph shows the elegant proportions of the Tickford-refined hood. Structurally it is largely the same as those fitted to the last MGB roadsters, although the fabric is superior and one or two other minor improvements have been made. *(Rover)*

Below: The MG RV8 was unveiled for the first time in public at the October 1992 Birmingham Motor Show, forming the centrepiece of the entire Rover stand. This photograph was taken on Press Day, shortly after the official unveiling by Rover Managing Director John Towers. *(David Knowles)*

Right: The interior of the RV8 would not look out of place in a Bentley or a Jaguar — it is certainly a world away from that of the original MGB GT V8. The elegant but rather impractical interior trim colour of Stone Beige is the only one available. (Autocar & Motor)

Right: The engine bay of the RV8 is completely filled by the mammoth 3.9-litre fuel injected Range Rover V8 engine. Note the remote air intake filter at the front nearside of the engine bay and the shroud over the radiator grille, an idea which Don Hayter would have introduced on the factory MGB GT V8 had he had the chance! Note also on this production car (K12 MGR) the black enamelled plenum chamber with the MG octagon. (Autocar & Motor)

Below: The RV8's specially-tooled rear lamp cluster was certainly worth its considerable cost, as can be seen in this three-quarter rear view shot. Some commentators have remarked on the resemblance of the rear wings to those of the Bentley Continental. (Rover)

Above: This beautifully executed ghosted view shows the relative positions of the engine, transmission and suspension. (Rover)

Below: Here the RV8 is shown with two record-breaking MGs from Abingdon's postwar years, EX-179 and EX-181. Both these remarkable vehicles form part of the British Motor Heritage Collection in Gaydon, Warwickshire. (Rover)

Opposite page
The glistening properties of the pearlescent Nightfire Red paint. are shown to the full in this beautifully composed shot. It is one of two standard pearlescents, the other being Caribbean Blue. (Autocar & Motor)
Inset: The Nightfire Red RV8 has been tested by a large number of publications, including Autocar & Motor, British Cars and What Car?, and on BBC Television's Top Gear programme. These atmospheric photographs were taken by Stan Papior, Autocar & Motor's skilled photographer. (Autocar & Motor)

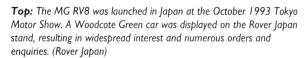

Top: The MG RV8 was launched in Japan at the October 1993 Tokyo Motor Show. A Woodcote Green car was displayed on the Rover Japan stand, resulting in widespread interest and numerous orders and enquiries. (Rover Japan)

Above: The first 46 RV8s were shipped to Japan on January the 13th, 1994. Here they are pictured lined up at Southampton Docks prior to loading on the Wallenius Lines vessel, Don Carlos. (Andrew Roberts)

Above and below: RV8s being loaded into the hold of the Don Carlos. Note the protective hood cover, lack of front fog lamps, temporary adhesive bump strips, chrome 'Rover' script on the front wing and slight lip around front wheelarches, the last two features unique to the Japanese-specification cars. Lower picture shows the cars stowed and secured and awaiting departure. (Andrew Roberts)

5

The MGB GT V8 in Competition

The Factory and The V8

In a contemporary report on the MGB GT V8 for the *Daily Telegraph*, Motoring Correspondent John Langley wondered if British Leyland might be tempted to campaign the car against the Datsun 240Z, which was so successful in the tough East African rallies during the early 1970s. Sadly, however, there was no prospect of the car being campaigned officially, since British Leyland's management saw no merit in the idea. They preferred at that time to focus their efforts on saloon models, and before very long they would concentrate their sports car competition budget on the Triumph TR7, for which they had high hopes.

The TR7, ironically enough, would be prepared at the Abingdon Competitions Department. Although there would, of course, be a great deal of enthusiasm and pride in the work which would subsequently be carried out on these cars by MG staff, there would inevitably be an undercurrent of resentment. Even a small part of the money to be spent on the Triumphs could have gone a long way towards campaigning MGs.

The story of the factory campaigning of the MGB GT V8, therefore, is that there is really no story to tell. To Don Hayter and others, this is a matter of eternal regret, as they believed it would have been the ideal car for MG to campaign. However, its potential was not overlooked by others. Over the years, the V8 has been raced, rallied and hillclimbed, always with distinction and always in the hands of 'privateers' — though sometimes, it must be said, with surreptitious backing from Abingdon.

The MG Car Club BCV8 Championship — by Brian Halford

The MG Car Club has for almost 20 years run a racing championship especially for the MGB, MGC and V8. In more recent times, this has benefited from the generous patronage of the largest supplier and manufacturer of MG spares in the world — MOSS Europe. The MOSS Europe MGCC BCV8 Championship is a national series run on circuits all over Britain, and including invitation races in Belgium and Holland. Such is the popularity of 'BCV8' that even during the recessionary years of the early 'nineties it has still been able to attract close to one hundred competitors, often necessitating the splitting of the four-class Championship into two races.

The origins of the Championship lie in the summer of 1976 when it was jointly conceived by Victor Smith and well-known MGB racer and current BCV8 President Barry Sidery Smith. Two years later it gained formal recognition. Prominent among the famous names who have competed in the Championship are the 1990 British Touring Car Champion Rob Gravett, who cut his teeth on MGs and won the BCV8 Championship in 1987; Gerry Marshall, who has driven in virtually every category of National racing; and David Franklin (the Steigenberger Hotels Supersports Champion in his McLaren M6B) who has driven his MGB GT V8 regularly in the Championship and won it in 1981. Lola T70 GT driver Terry Smith is also a former champion.

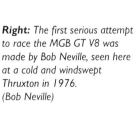

Right: *The first serious attempt to race the MGB GT V8 was made by Bob Neville, seen here at a cold and windswept Thruxton in 1976.*
(Bob Neville)

As presently constituted, the Championship is divided into four classes:

Class A: For standard MGBs and MGCs with virtually no modifications. Road tyres are used and the few modifications which are allowed are those deemed necessary for safety reasons and are generally confined to suspension and brakes. Many competitors start out in this class, which demands relatively little financial outlay and allows them to drive their racing MGs to the circuit. Class A is usually the most popular category and frequently provides exciting and closely contested motor racing.

Class B: For standard MGB GT V8s and for road-going MGBs and MGCs which are allowed greater freedom of tuning, especially to the engine. New for 1993 were the 'Sebring Replica' MGC GTs, resembling the last MGs raced by the Abingdon works. Class B provides a convenient stepping-stone between the standard and full-race classes.

Class C: Allows almost unlimited modifications to MGB and MGC engine, body, suspension and brake components. This class represents the ultimate race evolution of the four- and six-cylinder MG. In 1993 use of a 'limited modified' V8 engine was introduced, largely in response to the heavy costs incurred by the highly-tuned four- and six-cylinder units. Class C cars are lighter than those in Classes A and B and on some circuits are able to challenge some of the Class D competitors.

Class D: For full-modified V8-engined cars which are otherwise similar to Class C and, like Class C, running on slick tyres. With the 3.9-litre Rover-based engines producing over 300bhp, these cars have impressive performance and are spectacular to watch. The regulations allow the V8 engine to be installed in an MGB or MGC roadster or GT bodyshell.

The Privateers

Bob Neville, one of the development team at Abingdon at the time of the V8 launch, started racing in 1967 and, through his exploits in the ex-Roger Enever Midget, 138 DMO, was soon a force to be reckoned with. Keen to exploit the potential of the most powerful MG, in May 1973 Neville decided to undertake the preparation of an MGB GT V8 for racing, initially in MG Car Club races, with John Bilton, a senior BL executive.

Neville soon laid down the bare bones of the significantly lightened and uprated car. He obtained a Rover 3.5 race engine and this was built and prepared by Cliff Humphries, the engine builder in the Abingdon Competitions Department. The car itself was prepared personally by Neville, with bodywork by

Mark Hale of the MG panel shop. Bearing in mind Abingdon's long and distinguished involvement with competition, it is hardly surprising that a goodly number of talented MG people, such as Don Hayter, Terry Mitchell, Barry Jackson, Henry Stone, Cliff Bray, Geoff Clarke and Rodney Line, were soon lending their assistance to the project.

Its first outing, where it started from pole position, was at an MG Car Club race at Silverstone, in 1975. Neville's early endeavours centred on the popular grass-roots Modsports races, but the arrival of the Group 5 World Sportscar Championship in 1976 led to a change of tack and the car was soon being extensively reworked in readiness for the Silverstone six-hour race on May the 29th, 1976. Driven by Neville and Bob Worthington, the V8 qualified 24th but was soon powering its way up among the leaders, among which were such fearsome competitors as the Porsche 935 and BMW 3.5CSL, with such drivers as Mass, Ickx and Walkinshaw at the wheel.

By the halfway stage, it was apparent that barring any major calamity the V8 was destined for a highly honourable first Championship outing. (Neville recalls being approached by the excited BRDC Clerk of the Course, Pierre Aumonier, who told him that the car need only maintain its position to finish in the points.) In the event, it finished eighth, two places ahead of the Mass/Ickx Porsche, thus winning the last-ever World Championship points for MG.

As a result of this success, Neville was called in to help with a project being pursued by the Stratstone Group. In 1977 he sold his car to Malcolm Beer, who has campaigned it ever since.

The **Stratstone** MGB GT V8 racer was prepared in 1976 for an onslaught on the European racing scene. Stratstone, major distributors and dealers of British Leyland vehicles, decided to develop and race a highly modified version of the car in a number of international modified sports car races, the leading competition at the time being the celebrated Martini Porsches.

The car Stratstone bought was originally owned by Mike Gidden, who had commissioned Chas Beattie Projects of West London to design and prepare it for him, with the task of engine preparation being given to Weslake Engineering. In

Stratstone guise, the car was finished distinctively in their colours of dark blue and gold. Its sponsors included Leyland Cars — the nearest thing to official recognition of a competition MGB GT V8.

The engine capacity was enlarged to 3.9 litres, presaging the new RV8 by some 16 years. Isky camshafts, a four-choke Holley carburettor and an Offenhauser manifold were employed. Cosworth pistons were adopted and the ignition was provided by AC Delco, whose alternator was already a familiar fitment on road cars. Transmission was through the standard MGB GT V8 gearbox, an obvious weak link in the chain.

The body of the Stratstone car was a much lightened but otherwise standard MGB GT monocoque, though various aerodynamic aids were fitted and front and rear wheel arches were substantially enlarged. Rear suspension was basically standard MGB but with Beattie trailing links, whilst the front end featured Beattie wide-based wishbones, a tubular anti-roll bar, McLaren magnesium uprights and coil springs over adjustable dampers. Braking was by 10-inch ventilated discs of Beattie's own design, with Lockheed four-piston callipers at the front. At the back end, standard MGB drums were retained.

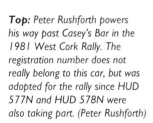

Top: Peter Rushforth powers his way past Casey's Bar in the 1981 West Cork Rally. The registration number does not really belong to this car, but was adopted for the rally since HUD 577N and HUD 578N were also taking part. (Peter Rushforth)

Right: Brian Field driving the lhd prototype GD2D2-97G through typically spectacular scenery during the 1977 International Welsh Rally.
(Foster & Skeffington)

Left: Field and his wife pose alongside their veteran MGB GT V8 rally car during the 1993 Haynes/Classic & Sportscar Tour. (Brian Field/Speedsports,Ruthin)

Below: Field at Clumber Park on his way to outright victory in the Mike Spence Historic Rally This event was run ahead of the RAC Rally, as is today's Britannia Historic. (Brian Field)

Bottom: Rae Davis of West London-based Motobuild is a seasoned campaigner in this MGB GT V8. (Autocar)

Right: Typical action from an MG Car Club BCV8 Championship race in the mid-1980s: two V8s lead an MGC roadster. (Autocar)

Below: Probably the best known MGB GT V8 racing today is the ex-Bob Neville car, which has been successfully campaigned by Malcolm Beer since 1976. It is still the car to beat in present day BCV8 Championship races. (Autocar)

Bottom: MG racers all. Pictured left to right are Rod Longton, Paul Campfield, Malcolm Beer, Peter Blackbourn, Colin Pearcy, Chris O'Neil and Tim Ransom. The occasion was the October 1986 Birkett six-hour relay race at Silverstone, where Peter Blackbourn was the manager. The photograph was taken by Neville Marriner, a V8 racer who is also a professional photographer with the Daily Mail. (Neville Marriner, courtesy Rod Longton)

Left: *Rod Longton's purposeful-looking V8 racer was built by Beer of Houghton, using an old GT bodyshell and a full-race ex-Rallycross 3.5 litre engine. Longton had several good races in it, including 2nd at Thruxton and Brands Hatch and 5th at Spa, prior to selling it in 1991. The car raced in some 40 races without the engine being touched, which must be something of a record! (Rod Longton)*

Below: *Longton's V8 racer in action at the famous 'bus stop' on the Spa racing circuit… (Rod Longton)*

Employed by Stratstone's principal driver, Tim Goss, to help sort the car, Bob Neville was confined to test-driving for a time but later participated with Goss in two International World Championship events — at Silverstone in May 1977, where they failed to finish, and at Brands Hatch in September 1977, where in appallingly wet conditions they came in 16th.

Following these two outings, which left them out of the points but gained them valuable exposure, Stratstone decided to bring their involvement with the car to an end; it was sold to Richard Scantlebury, who continued to campaign it in lower-key national events. In August 1978, during the BRSCC Mallory Park weekend, Scantlebury held off a powerful line-up of Aston Martins to win the all-comers race.

At the age of seventeen and only two days after passing his driving test, **Malcolm Beer** won the very first race he entered. The car was an ultra-rare MG Q-Type which had raced at Brooklands, and the year and venue of this distinguished debut were 1965 at Brands Hatch. Since then, Beer has driven a wide variety of MGs, including his Jacobs Midget, Modsports Midgets, a K3 Magnette, a Metro, an MGB, and the car he is perhaps best known for, the ex-Bob Neville MGB GT V8, which he acquired in 1977. It was in this car that he competed in the first official BCV8 race that year and, apart from a change of allegiance to a roadster in 1987, he has driven it in the BCV8 Championship ever since. He remains one of the most formidable competitors in the field and is frequently to be seen in the paddock passing on the benefits of his experience to others.

Another distinguished competition career is that of Cardiff-based **Brian Field**, who began rallying his V8 upon his

retirement in 1974 and has never looked back. Field visited Abingdon in 1974 with the intention of obtaining one of the V8-powered cars at a reasonable price; he already possessed a Rover V8 engine and was hoping to acquire a suitable bodyshell and build up a Group 4 rally car which would serve for hillclimbing, racing and road use. However, after speaking to the people at MG, he realised that the notion of attempting to campaign a single car in two different categories had little to recommend it, and consequently decided to prepare two cars. MG then offered him two of the lhd prototype V8s, shorn of their doors and various mechanical equipment, at the knockdown price of £1,000 (plus road tax) the pair. These were Harvest Gold 97 (a pre-production lhd car) and Glacier White 102 (the second production V8, now owned by Dutchman Bas Geritts and featured elsewhere in this book). Field bought both cars, but soon found the commitment more than he could handle. He prepared the white car (HUD 578N) for road use and sold it to Peter Rushforth, who subsequently sold it to Michael Pearson-Kirk.

With only one car to worry about, Field found himself out on a limb, since the factory had built up absolutely no competition expertise with the V8s. The small measure of help Abingdon provided was reinforced by various tuning experts in the USA, home of the Buick/Rover engine, but for the most part Field and his mechanic were obliged to improvise. All the special V8 prototype parts (including the lhd steering set-up) and the twin SU carburettors were removed and laid aside for restoration after the car's retirement from racing. Rebuilt and equipped with the ubiquitous Holley carburettor, Offenhauser manifold and mandatory safety equipment, the V8 was ready to compete by May 1975. Field at once entered the 1975 International Welsh Rally, achieving a creditable third in class and winning one stage.

Encouraged by this success, the Field team set their sights higher and prepared for an assault on the RAC Rally. A number of fundamental changes were made to the rear suspension, including the fabrication of rear turrets for telescopic dampers and springs. The service crew was made up of enthusiastic MG Car Club members and the car took a terrific pounding over the gruelling event, but still managed a stage win at Longleat and a final placing of 92nd out of 250.

On the 1975 Scottish Rally, the car started well but was brought to a disappointingly premature halt by a gearbox fault

Above: ...and at Brands Hatch in 1990, fending off a challenge from fellow BCV8 competitor Steve Williams.
(Chris Harvey, courtesy Rod Longton)

Right: Mike Breedon returned to racing in the BCV8 Championship in 1993 after a brief lay-off. His immaculate MGB GT V8, TAN 926M, demonstrates that it is possible to race the cars and still use them on the road.
(Brian Halford)

Right: At the other end of the BCV8 spectrum is this car, painstakingly rebuilt to full race V8 specification by Stephen Ratcliffe. It is seen here in 1993, in its first race for three years, with Richard Finney at the wheel. The car was formerly owned by photographer Neville Marriner and was raced by him in 1989.
(Brian Halford)

Left: *In the foreground in this 1992 picture is Roy McCarthy in his pristine yellow Class D MGB GT V8, which is the ex-Richard Horn 'Oselli' car. Behind him, in the ex-Bob Neville V8, is 1991 Championship winner Malcolm Beer. (Brian Halford)*

— though there was some compensation for this when driver and navigator won a gallon of Scotch at the post-rally party!

Since those early endeavours, the Harvest Gold V8 has shone in numerous events, registering several outright wins and many class wins. Field was able to register the car with the Historic Rally Car Club, by virtue of the fact that it had been manufactured in 1972 and had acquired a distinguished rally record. In recent years it has been extensively developed and now features a Salisbury rear axle, gas-filled adjustable spring/damper units and Minilite wheels. By 1993, Field was concentrating primarily on 'Post Historic' events — in deference, as he puts it, to his advancing years.

A contemporary of Brian Field's in the rallies of the late 'seventies and early 'eighties was **Peter Rushforth,** the man who bought one of the two cars which Field had purchased from MG. In 1977, in fact, Rushforth and **Michael Pearson-Kirk** each owned 50 percent of the car, though Rushforth later relinquished his half-share. HUD 578N competed alongside Field's Harvest Gold warhorse in the 1977 International Welsh Rally, from which both cars emerged with credit. Rushforth subsequently bought a second V8 from Derek Skinner and competed successfully in it, including an entry in the 1981 West Cork Rally where the car bore the false number HUD 576N (actually the number of another lhd V8 currently owned by Gerhard Maier, in Germany). Afterwards the car was re-registered as KBW 485N, the number which it bears to this day.

HUD 578N, meanwhile, was rallied with some vigour by Pearson-Kirk, who also modified it extensively, fitting it with a Holley carburettor and various other non-standard parts. Eventually the car was sold on, passing through several changes of ownership before travelling first to Sweden and finally to Holland.

Rod Longton will happily admit to having started serious racing over 40 years ago, beginning in 1953 with a 2.4-litre Riley. Longton, a retired GP from Epping, Essex, remained faithful to the Riley marque with his next car, a 1.5 saloon which he subsequently fitted with a Stage V MGB race engine. This engine was sufficiently successful that it was used in his next two cars, successively an Elva Courier and a TVR 1800 MkIII. It was in the latter that Longton came equal first with Roger Enever in the Amasco Racing Championship run at the tail-end of the 1960s.

The TVR was sold in 1970 and was instantly replaced by another, this time a Tuscan, which won the STP Modsports Championship. Then in 1973 Longton took a long sabbatical from racing until, six years later, he purchased an MGB and

began a long association with the MG Car Club BCV8 Championship. Registered 3373 MZ, the MGB was a 1963 car, prepared for racing in Northern Ireland during the 1960s by Archie Phillips and raced first by Norman Conn and then by Rod McDowall, from whom Longton purchased it. It was raced as a full-race 1800 until 1984, when Longton converted it to V8 power with an engine built by Martin Thomas at SRG (later to be replaced by an ex-Colin Pearcy Swindon unit). After four enjoyable years, Longton sold the V8 to Bill Beadnell, of DAF Trucks. Beadnell, racing with Bob Berridge, installed a JE Motors engine in the car, in which form it became one of the quickest MGB racers around — and certainly one of the ugliest!

Longton's next car was a green MGB GT which, as he tells it, he acquired almost by accident. He owned at that time an old MGB GT rolling bodyshell, which he had purchased for less than £100. A local garage owner and rallycross enthusiast named John White, having decided to turn his back on the sport, offered Longton a full-race 3.5 works development engine, built by RS Engineering, which had clocked up only two events. Not surprisingly, this seemed to Longton the perfect opportunity to build a 'low-cost' MGB V8 racer — and, with the best of everything poured into it, including Sebring-style bodywork by Beer of Houghton, the car won the accolade of 'Best Turned-out V8 in BCV8 Racing for 1990' — having cost its owner a total of £13,000!

Longton enjoyed a great deal of rewarding racing in the car, including second places at Thruxton and Brands Hatch and fifth at Spa, before selling it to Derek Stewart in 1991. Between the two drivers the car managed 40 races without any need to touch the engine, which is surely a testament to the strength of the Rover V8 unit and must surely be a record in its own right. Stewart rebuilt the car in 1993 and even managed to beat Malcolm Beer in one race — quite an achievement!

Longton's latest car, AVU 900T, was bought from Bob Slesser in 1992 as a half-finished MGB V8 project and was converted to a 1950cc Class C racer. In 1993, however, with the introduction of the new Class C V8s marking the arrival of the RV8, Longton decided to go V8 once more. The car was fitted with a 3.9-litre engine with limited tune and a TVR bell-housing mated with a Ford Sierra Cosworth gearbox. Painted black and yellow, it resembles Longton's first MGB racer. The letters DEJ have been neatly painted on the rear bodywork, to the left of the number plate; hence its nickname of *Déja Vu*. Certain to be out and about on the race-tracks in 1994 and beyond, Longton in *Déja Vu* will remain a major force in BCV8 circles.

6

Rebirth:
The MG RV8

The Heritage Connection

The story of the RV8 starts, of course, with the introduction of the Heritage MGB bodyshell at the Faringdon
facility, masterminded by former Cowley body engineer David
Bishop. However, the roots of the car are more closely
entwined with Heritage than through the bodyshell alone.

During a visit to the then-new Faringdon premises in 1988,
the author, along with other V8 Register members, asked
about the possibility of a V8 roadster bodyshell being made
available — an almost inevitable question, bearing in mind the
growing number of MGBs which were by then being converted to V8 power. Previously David Bishop had always
maintained that the purpose of the Heritage MGB bodyshell
was solely to provide a 'service replacement' for the owners
of existing rusty MGBs. On this occasion, though, he confessed
to having recognised that it would eventually be necessary to
consider a V8 shell, even though such a specification had never
been developed at Abingdon. Already, in fact, Bishop and some
of his colleagues were toying with the idea of producing a
complete MGB V8 roadster. Roger Parker, the V8 Register's
knowledgeable V8 Roadster Representative, had built a
remarkably sophisticated fuel-injected example which, as
described in Chapter Eight, had made a most favourable
impression at a Rover management meeting.

*Right: The prime force behind
the rebirth of the MGB bodyshells, without which there would,
of course, have been no MG
RV8, is British Motor Heritage
Managing Director David Bishop,
seen here in conversation with
V8 Register members during a
visit to the bodyshell facility at
Faringdon. (David Knowles)*

Much work was carried out in examining the feasibility of
producing what would effectively have been a brand-new
1970s-style V8 roadster. Former MG personnel, including
Don Hayter, Terry Mitchell and Cliff Humphries, were contacted and consulted. A source from outside the company told
the author that the intended price of the car was understood
to be well below that of the RV8 — even as low as £17,000
— though of course it would have lacked much of the
sophistication of the car which eventually emerged. Two

*Right: One of the earliest
purpose-built MGB V8 roadsters
which used a British Motor
Heritage MGB bodyshell as its
basis was this fine specimen built
by Trevor Taylor. With its
chrome wire wheels, traditional
chrome-finished MG radiator
grille and chrome bumpers, it
suggests how the 'Heritage MGB
V8' might have looked had it
ever emerged. (Trevor Taylor)*

Left: Stored behind the British Motor Heritage facility at Faringdon are many tons of salvaged press tools, for such vehicles as Triumph TR6s, GT6s and Spitfires, as well as MG Midgets and MGBs. Each one of these tools has been carefully logged and, where necessary, reconditioned. (David Knowles)

Bottom: Lined up at Rover's top-secret research and testing establishment at Gaydon, Warwickshire, are (left to right); YWU 486S, known as DEV 2, the second RV8 development vehicle, based on an MGB bodyshell and used primarily for cooling tests; KAE 868P, a Bracken 1975 MGB GT V8, bought for comparison, testing and development purposes; JGT 808N, the third development car built on an MGB bodyshell. Car magazine included a 'spy shot' of this car in its June 1992 issue. (John Yea, Rover Special Products)

prototypes were built, using original bodyshells. The first of these, known as DEV 1, was a left-hand-drive US-specification MGB (registered LFC 436S), from British Motor Heritage's vast collection of vehicles. This car was fitted with a new 3.5-litre Rover engine from the Land Rover factory at Solihull. BMH's Mark Gamble was put in charge of turning the MGB into a V8 in the spring of 1990, and the work was carried out in much the same way as in many private conversions, along the lines described in Chapter Eight.

Appearance was not a priority at this juncture. As Gamble put it: 'We fitted the engine into the shell with our own fabricated mountings, which meant of course that the standard Lucas injection unit projected through the bonnet. We overcame this problem by cutting a hole in the bonnet and covering it with a biscuit tin!' This car was eventually used as the basis for a styling model, with cosmetic plastic parts built into the original bodywork, and it was subsequently used as the basis of the 'teaser' brochure issued in advance of the RV8 launch. The car still survives, but is not structurally sound and most certainly not roadworthy!

The second car, which resided until recently at Rover's Gaydon test facility, but was eventually sold, was based on a brand-new rubber-bumper MGB bodyshell which David Bishop located. Finished in red and registered as YWU 486S, this car was fitted with a 3.9-litre Rover V8 engine and significantly uprated suspension — a precursor of the set-up which would ultimately emerge in the RV8. After much heart-searching, Heritage Chairman Les Wharton decided that the potential pitfalls and sheer volume of work required to bring the car to production were too great to justify and that

Heritage's efforts would be better applied to their core business of servicing the classic car market, leaving actual car manufacture to Rover. However, the groundwork had already been carried out, so that when the project was taken on by Rover the prospects of it reaching production were virtually assured — with an active role retained for Heritage in the production of the bodyshell.

The Rover V8 Engine — Into the 1990s

The Rover V8 engine has had a truly remarkable history, stretching back well over 30 years. Although its use in main-stream Rover saloon products ended when the last Rover SD1 was built in the mid-1980s, its application to a number of very successful products of the Rover Group's Land Rover division has ensured its survival since then.

There was a time when the future of relatively large-capacity V8 engines looked bleak; in fact the launch of the Rover SD1 and Triumph TR8 on the North American market at the end of the 1970s could not have come at a worse time, since it seemed then that the Americans were finally turning away from the engine layout which they had made their own. In 1978, for example, the installation rate for V8 engines in US domestic cars was 67 percent, compared with a high of 83 percent in 1973; only just above 16 percent of all cars sold in the USA in 1978 were fitted with V8 engines, about half the figure for the previous year.

Fortunately this trend slowed somewhat as the 1980s progressed, and the application of V8 engines to more luxur-ious vehicles regained popularity in a market where fuel was

still relatively cheap. The launch of the Range Rover into the North American market in 1987 was something of a master stroke by the company, and with the work which had already been carried out on ensuring that the V8 met US vehicle emissions requirements, the task of ensuring that the Range Rover would comply was made simpler (and more economically feasible) than a 'clean sheet' exercise would have been.

The launch of the Land Rover Discovery, which uses the 3.5- and 3.9-litre fuel-injected V8, and the application of the engine to the traditional Land Rover (now renamed the Land Rover Defender) has meant that the V8 engine remains a fairly permanent fixture in the Rover cupboard, so the application of a very mildly uprated 3.9 V8 to the low-volume MG RV8 project was again comparatively easy: the only significant alterations needed were cosmetic changes to the plenum chamber casting and a different camshaft. The Land Rover Discovery shares the MG RV8's ex-Rover SD1 five-speed gearbox, so Rover did not need to look outside the company for an in-line rear-wheel-drive gearbox, despite the fact that there are currently no rear-wheel-drive Rover saloon cars.

The V8 engine is still manufactured at Acocks Green, as it has been from the earliest days, and with the launch of an all-new Range Rover imminent, including some very exciting developments of the classic alloy unit planned for the top versions, it is certain to outlive the RV8. Perhaps we shall even see it in another all-new MG sports car one day?

Emergence of the RV8

Once BMH had concluded that the production of a complete car was outside their sphere of operations, the idea was taken up by the newly-formed Rover Special Products team. RSP began researching the project in April 1991, starting with a survey of market groups which they believed would be most likely to respond to the car. According to RSP Director Steve Schlemmer, the most probable potential customers were those who were affluent (naturally!), middle-aged, and likely to recall with nostalgia the era of open MG sports cars, even though they may not have been owners themselves.

The first vehicle which could properly be described as an RV8 development car was built in the autumn of 1991 and was little more than a kit of parts assembled in a Heritage MGB bodyshell. It had a Land Rover fuel-injected V8 installed, coupled to the familiar Rover 77mm in-line gearbox. At no stage was any serious consideration given to any other power unit: not only had the V8 been proved to work well in the MGB body, but also it was perceived as having the right credentials for an expensive sporting car and, furthermore, it would be easier to certify for production than an engine which had not previously been used in the MGB.

The RV8 was designed from the outset to take advantage of as much existing MGB hardware as possible, yet the finished product was to contain only five percent original MGB components. The vast majority of parts, including engine, drivetrain, electrical system, body and trim, are all either totally new or adapted from other Rover products. Many of the parts which had been used in the MGB were no longer in production, or were available only in reconditioned form, or were simply deemed unsuitable for a 1990s car.

The suspension is a case in point, since the original MGB V8 used the already outdated Armstrong lever arm dampers to provide the upper wishbone at the front, with very stiff multiple-leaf 'cart springs' fitted at the rear. The RV8's re-designed suspension comprises a modified MGB front

Top: This cutaway of a 3.9 litre Range Rover V8 clearly shows the injectors, plenum chamber and valve train of the classic unit in its latest version. (Rover)
Above: Each V8 engine is meticulously prepared at the Acocks Green engine facility, using state-of-the-art equipment. (Rover)

Below: The rear lamp clusters of the RV8 neatly incorporate the reversing lights (which were separate units on the MGB GT V8) and a more modern, rounded shape. Although they were very expensive to tool up, the result has clearly been worthwhile as they are one of the most universally admired features of the new car. (David Knowles)

Left: The nose of the MG RV8 is equally distinctive, for it incorporates a neat updating of the original MGB theme. The complex all-in-one steel wing of the MGB was difficult and expensive to produce to a high enough standard, so a separate reinforced plastic headlamp nascelle has been adopted to house the slightly raked back unit. (David Knowles)

Below: The 15in spoked alloy wheels echo the wire wheels of the original MGB. The neat octagonal cap with its bronze-and-cream MG badge makes a handsome centrepiece. (David Knowles)

Aside from the choice of 'solid' or 'pearlescent' paint finish, the only other factory-fitted option available at the launch was a compact disc player with auto-change unit, mounted in the boot. With the RV8 bootlid being virtually identical to that of the MGB, it is a strong possibility that a luggage-rack will be offered as a dealer-fitted option; there are of course several high-quality racks already available. A further option, which many owners will regard as essential and which Rover are currently considering, is a full tonneau cover to protect the interior from light rain showers when parked with the hood down.

Overall, while maintaining obvious links with the MGB, the RV8 has been given a much more aggressive 'muscular' stance, appropriate to its performance. Furthermore, the standard of finish and the upmarket character of the interior are of course considerably higher than those to which most owners of the original MGB would ever have aspired.

In conversation with the author, Steve Schlemmer was keen to point out that the goal had *not* been to produce the 'ultimate' sports car; rather, development had been concentrated on making the RV8 as safe and enjoyable as possible, in the tradition of its Abingdon ancestors.

The Faringdon RV8 Body Facility

The RV8 body facility at Faringdon is the latest extension of this growing mecca for MG enthusiasts, situated on a small industrial estate barely a mile from the ancient market town centre. The facility is dedicated to the production of both RV8 and MGB bodies, the latter being periodically produced in small batches rather than alongside the RV8 bodies. Production of RV8 bodies began in the autumn of 1992, when the first of some 28 pre-production and development cars were built. The RV8 programme was christened 'Project ADDER' within Rover, and this name is still used at Faringdon as the familiar term for the RV8, appearing on notices and in documents throughout the facility.

The main framing jigs for the MGB and RV8 are common, and much of the structure uses a sensible amalgam of chrome-bumper and rubber-bumper MGB components. Heritage experienced a number of difficulties during development — for example, the need to provide adequate clearance between the bonnet bulge and the injection plenum chamber, between the steering rack and body members (a familiar problem to MGB GT V8 owners and would be V8 converters!) and a number of panel-fit problems. Rover personnel are often on hand to ensure that panel fits (including panel gaps) and finish are of sufficiently high standard for a high-priced motor car; what was acceptable ten or more years ago is clearly no longer good enough. The front cross-member, pressed in-house at Faringdon, required some alterations to suit the coil-over-shock front suspension set-up of the RV8, and David Bishop is justifiably proud of the design solution adopted by the team.

Early RV8 bodies were, of course, crash-tested and it was found that the shells remained supremely strong. Alterations made during development had been minimal, in the interests of complying with certification requirements, but even so it had been found necessary to add a few holes in order to help with the anti-corrosion treatment, which is carried out at Cowley on the completed ex-Faringdon shells. (David Bishop recalls that one of these holes, injudicially positioned, caused a minor deformation of the sill upon impact, and was consequently relocated.) In fact, the RV8 shell is better than the best of the original MGBs — the chrome-bumper cars — and is so

cross-member with a 'coil-over-shock' spring set-up with modern Koni telescopic dampers, whilst the rear suspension uses double-taper springs and appropriate fore/aft restraints fixed to massive brackets at the front leaf-spring mounting to prevent the axle-tramp which could afflict the old MGB GT V8 during hard acceleration.

MGC enthusiasts may be interested to know that the RV8's spoked alloy wheels are also 15in in diameter, although the tyres of course are wider and of much lower profile.

Some of the original MGB's components were less than adequate even when the car was in production and inevitably had to be replaced. For example, the heater unit used in the RV8 was specially developed using Mini and Metro components, and is reputedly so effective that Rover are thinking of offering it as an accessory to MGB owners. There is also talk of an optional air-conditioning unit, in response to requests from Japan.

Under the bonnet is Land Rover's 3.9-litre fuel-injected version of the venerable alloy V8. The two stainless steel exhaust manifolds disappear out of the engine bay via large reinforced holes in the inner wing panels, leading into twin catalytic converters tucked tightly away on each side of the transmission. It has been suggested that when the engine is used to the full, these converters virtually render the new heater redundant!

strong that the same shell was used for both the final front and the rear impact tests!

The RV8 uses a number of hand-pressed panels, made by Abbey Panels, whose other customers include Rolls-Royce (Corniche) and Jaguar (XJ220). Unlike the Jaguar XJ220, however, where the panels are made to fit on a highly labour-intensive basis, the RV8 panels have to be correct prior to painting, since the shells go through the new Cowley paint system (along with the Rover 600 and 800) and therefore have to be as near-perfect as possible beforehand. In the days when Heritage were chiefly concerned with MGB bodyshell production, nine staff were required to produce 16 to 17 bodies per week. With the new RV8 requiring 13 people to produce at the rate of 15 per week, David Bishop has already increased his staff by two and is likely to add more in the future.

Midget and TR6 bodyshell production was held up by the need to get the RV8 operation under way, but it is Bishop's firm intention to re-commence producing them as soon as possible. They remain a vital part of Heritage's core business, and Heritage are acutely aware of the need to avoid upsetting potential customers for them. The MGB bodyshells have gained enormously from the new technology and improvements brought about by the RV8 project: all MGB bodies are now produced using rust-resistant zinc-finished steel and MGB front wing production has been brought in-house, enabling Heritage to have better control over the quality and fit of these items — a welcome development, since they had previously been a common cause of complaint.

Production of RV8 bodies started at 12 per week, although this was gradually increased to 16 in order to exceed Cowley's requirement of 15 per week. Bishop's intention was that every fifteenth week production of MGB bodies would resume for one week: the switch from MGB to RV8 bodyshell production (or vice versa) can apparently be achieved in less than half an hour! The need to finish the shells to a very high paint-ready standard has necessitated the take-over of yet another unit on the Pioneer Road estate, expressly for the purpose of inspecting and hand-detailing each finished shell, before oil coating. Finished shells are transported 15 at a time to the Cowley works, where they are taken straight into the Rover 600/800 painting facility for cleaning, dipping, priming and final painting.

When they began production of MGB bodyshells, Heritage employed a turbocharged generator to provide the high

ROVER SPECIAL PRODUCTS

Rover Special Products — RSP, for short — was set up as a new division of the Rover Group in January 1990 for the express purpose of researching, designing and bringing to pre-production stage selected 'niche' products, which could profitably be produced in much lower numbers than would normally be contemplated by a large manufacturer.

Special Products is a small, tight-knit unit drawn from across the Rover Group and comprising, under the directorship of Steve Schlemmer, no more than 40 personnel. At any one time, there are usually four or five significant projects under way.

RSP were responsible for the limited edition Mini-Cooper, which marked the return of the performance Mini; plans for its re-introduction had been on the boil for several years, but it took the singular resources of the Special Products division to bring the idea to fruition.

Other special programmes have included the work required to re-launch the Land Rover marque in the USA, in the form of the Land Rover Defender (to be followed, soon afterwards, by the Discovery); the limited edition Range Rover CSK; the Mini and Metro Cabriolets; and a limited edition Mini Cooper 'Silverstone' for the German market. By the autumn of 1993, RSP had carried through a total of 19 'product actions', generating an extra £70 million in revenue for the Rover Group.

Top: One of a number of development hacks used originally by Rover Special Products, this black RV8 prototype accumulated a high mileage in the interest of fully developing the car prior to full manufacture. It is seen here during a 'guest appearance' at a V8 Register British Motor Heritage factory visit. (David Knowles)

Right: Seated behind the wheel of this pre-production Le Mans Green RV8 in Rover's Canley Design Studios is Steve Schlemmer, the Director in charge of Rover Special Products. (David Knowles)

Above: The bodyshell of the MG RV8 is manufactured by hand at the British Motor Heritage production facility at Faringdon, Oxfordshire. Here the basic monocoque is being spot-welded while the constituent panels are held in a specially adapted jig. (John Brigden/British Motor Heritage)

Left: Here the front sub-assembly, including the engine bay and front bulkhead, is being welded together on one of the many jigs originally rescued by David Bishop of British Motor Heritage. (John Brigden/British Motor Heritage)

Bottom: Both front and rear wings of the RV8 are pressed by Abbey Panels. Whereas the MGB wing is all metal, the front end of that for the RV8 features a composite plastic nacelle around the headlamp. (David Knowles)

Opposite page
Top: The body of the MG RV8 is closely related to the MGB bodyshell which is also produced at Faringdon, and as such is very labour intensive to produce: there are no robots at British Motor Heritage! This view clearly shows the elegantly reshaped rear wings.
(John Brigden/British Motor Heritage)
Bottom: When this photograph was taken, final finishing of the RV8 bodies was still being carried out in the main production facility; another unit on the Pioneer Road Estate has since been taken over for the express purpose of final finishing and examination by a Rover Quality Inspector. (John Brigden/British Motor Heritage)

Above: David Bloomfield is the manager of the Faringdon production facility, having taken over from Jack Bellinger who retired in 1993. Bloomfield is also responsible for the production of many other products, including parts for MG Midgets, Triumph Spitfires and TR6s. (John Brigden/British Motor Heritage)

currents necessary for welding to Rover's stringent standards. With the introduction of zinc-coated steel components in the RV8 and latest MGB shells, even higher welding standards were required, as a result of which Bishop acquired a V12 unit which had formerly seen service as a standby at Cowley. Samples of the shell are regularly subjected to the torture of weld destruction tests, in which each spot weld is chiselled apart in order to verify its strength.

In conversation with the author, Bishop and former Manager Jack Bellinger (who retired in 1993 and whose shoes have been ably filled by David Bloomfield) stressed that virtually everything at Faringdon bar the main fabric of the buildings had been prepared by the staff themselves, not only reducing expense but also engendering a strong sense of pride in self-sufficiency throughout the entire workforce. Heritage, in common with Rover, has achieved the coveted BS5750 'Quality Accreditation', an externally audited assessment awarded only to those who meet the highest of standards.

RV8 Production At Cowley

Tucked away in a corner of the vast Cowley manufacturing complex is a smart cream building which holds a myriad of treasures for the MG enthusiast. High above the entrance is a sign proudly displaying the bronze-and-cream MG badge and the title 'RV8 Manufacturing Facility'. Conscious of the significance of the building for future historians, Rover also salvaged an elegant gold-and-black Morris Motors clock from the old Cowley South works — 'S Block' — demolished in 1993 and now the site of a new retail and office development.

Graham Irvine, Project Director in charge of the MG RV8 operation at Cowley, was responsible for taking the car from development prototype to finished product in less than a year. Irvine's team, led by Manufacturing Manager Cliff Law, were instructed to bring into production a car which shared none of the hardware of the current Rover car range, whilst keeping to a tight budget.

Starting on the first of August 1992, Irvine and a workforce which varied in number (up to 60 at one point) began sourcing the equipment, personnel and raw materials needed to carry out the appropriate design and production develop- ment. Fortunately, the Cowley team was able to salvage a good many manufacturing aids from the redundant South works, even down to roof beams and various assembly jigs and test equipment. Much of the fitting out and preparation of the facility was done by the staff themselves — a reflection of their enthusiasm for the task in hand and an effective team-building exercise into the bargain.

Irvine contrasts the philosophy of the RV8 facility with that of the more common large volume factories, such as the remainder of Cowley or the second main Rover car-manufacturing site at Longbridge: 'In Cowley's main 'A' Building or at Longbridge, a typical work cycle would be from three to five minutes; here each operator has about two and a half hours-worth of work to involve him at any one time.' A further advantage is the relative compactness of the RV8 facility: 'In the 'A' Building, where Rover 600s and 800s are built, the line is about a quarter of a mile long; but in the RV8 facility no one is ever more than thirty yards or so from the car.'

Each operative has developed a range of skills which enables him (or her) to carry out tasks beyond his normal sphere of operations, and Cliff Law foresees the time coming when each person could in theory build the entire car himself. As well as enabling operatives to cover for one another in the case of absence through holidays or sickness, this set-up has also (as has been similarly proved in other industries) helped the workers to identify with the product and fostered a strong sense of pride in seeing it through. Unlike the conventional sequence of events, where a car is developed behind closed doors by a team divorced from the actual production process, the RV8 and the 600 and 800 pilot cars were taken from scratch to final pre-production stage by the production workforce itself, with appropriate engineering guidance as necessary. As a solution to many of the problems encountered in the bad old days, when cars were often said to be 'designed by the customer', this is described succinctly by Irvine as a return to common sense.

The Cowley MG RV8 facility is, of course, no more than the tip of the iceberg, assembling the products of a number of other factories in a manner which in many ways parallels the old Abingdon factory, albeit on a smaller scale.

Bodyshells, at a rate of 15 per week, are delivered by road from the Faringdon facility to the main Rover 600/800 paint facility nearby, where the bare shells are electro-coated and primed to the same high standards which Rover demand for all of their current car range. The final colour and finishing coats are then applied before baking on and a number of small areas — such as the forward facing edge of the bonnet landing-platform support-bracket — are mask-sprayed matt black (for purely cosmetic reasons). The painted shells then pass through into the RV8 facility itself, and the final stages towards completion are set in motion.

Above: Some of the team behind the MG RV8 pose proudly with the car at the Cowley manufacturing facility. At the wheel is Rover Director John Towers, in the passenger seat is Steve Schlemmer (Managing Director of the Rover Special Products subsidiary). To the extreme left of the photo is the Plant Manager, Cliff Law, while just behind the passenger door mirror is Roy Belcher, who served at Abingdon for 26 years, right up until its closure in 1980. (Rover)

At Station One, following the removal and storage of the bonnet, the inner recesses of the bodyshell are pressure-treated with wax, reinforcing the ability of the high-technology zinc-treated steel of the body to resist the onslaught of corrosion. A few other minor jobs are also carried out at this point which would be more difficult at a later stage, such as the installation of the radio aerial. A Vehicle Identity Number (VIN) is allocated to the car, correlated to the Heritage body number and the various other unit numbers associated with it. The plate is temporarily tagged onto the front of the car, to be riveted into position at a later stage, and defines the legal identity of the car from this point on.

At Station Two, the complex wiring harness is installed by Elaine Butler, whose experience gained on the Rover 800 line stands her in good stead for this skilled task. Any restorer who has rebuilt an MG will appreciate what an impressive sight the installation of a complete loom in a matter of minutes makes! Various electrical components, including the headlights, are also installed at this stage. Elaine's enthusiasm for her work is infectious; interviewed for Rover's in-house newspaper, *Torque*, she declared: 'I think we've all fallen in love with this

car. It's more than a job and that's why we're all determined to get it absolutely right.'

At Station Three, the pre-assembled dashboard unit is carefully unpacked and fitted into the cockpit, with all the associated instruments and many of the trim items being installed. The various door and boot locks are installed at this point, the Range Rover-style remote control 'blipper' being tied to the front of the car to await installation of the steering column at a later stage. Noel Johnson and Steve Cook take about two hours to carry out this part of the process, and both are very happy with their work: Steve, who is rebuilding an MGB at home in his spare time, describes his work on the RV8 as 'much more satisfying' than his previous jobs at the factory, while for Noel the switch to the RV8 after 20 years at the plant came as a distinct but nonetheless welcome culture shock.

Work at Station Four includes the installation of the fuel tank (with high-pressure fuel pump and fuel lines), together with the boot compartment trim, the remaining lights and the windscreen. Transfer from here to Station Five involves the use of some specially adapted slings, previously used to carry Rover 800 bodies in the Cowley North works. In that role they had been fully automatic, but for the RV8 facility they were adapted to manually controlled electric power. The shell is then carefully lifted about eight feet into the air and is suspended over two axle tables — formerly used on the Maestro/Montego lines — where the complete front and rear axle assemblies are installed and the torque control arms are fixed to the sturdy brackets which are one of many small but significant changes from the old MGB bodyshell.

Above: The beautifully crafted dashboard is installed into the MG RV8 as a pre-assembled unit, but nevertheless requires careful handling and plumbing in. (David Knowles)

With axles and steering assembly installed, the body proceeds to Station Six where the engine and transmission assembly, carefully removed from its 'Adder cage', is lowered inch by inch into position. As anyone who has tried it will testify, this is a nerve-racking process, although the three-man team responsible make it look comparatively easy. (One of the three is Roy Belcher, who worked at Abingdon from 1954 to 1980 and is delighted to be part of MG history once more.)

At Station Seven, the final build takes place — including the last remaining items of interior trim — and oil, water and brake fluid are added, the introduction of coolant utilising a home-made filling device devised by the team to avoid air-locks.

Now able to move under its own power, the car is transferred to one of a number of test bays where the equivalent of an MOT is carried out: brake, emissions and lighting tests are performed, and wheel alignment is checked. The final body kit items, including the moulded front and rear bumper aprons and front grille surround, are installed on a ramp and a pre-road test is carried out to check for leakages from any of the gaskets or other components. This done, the car is then taken to the Rover 800 facility, where it is under-waxed before a full road test is carried out. The test route skirts southwards through the charismatically-named Oxfordshire village of Nuneham Courtenay, passing over a

variety of road surfaces to ensure that the car is up to scratch.

Following successful completion of the test, the car is returned to the RV8 building where it is fully valeted and hand wax-polished. It leaves the plant in showroom condition, rather than coated in wax, minimising the pre-delivery work required at the dealers and ensuring that the finish is as near perfect as possible. Cliff Law then contacts the despatch representatives who are invited to inspect the car — scrutinising it as a customer would — before agreeing to 'buy' it and then taking it away for a brief period of covered storage prior to despatch to the dealer by closed trailer.

The RV8 Unveiled

Although the RV8 was not shown to the public until the October 1992 Birmingham Motor Show, the issue of 'teaser' photos and of an advance brochure the previous June had already gained it widespread attention. The first non-company people actually to see the car was a group of about 20 representatives of Britain's two main MG Car Clubs (including the author) and the leading UK- and USA-based MG enthusiast publications. The viewing took place on Wednesday, September the 16th, 1992, little more than a month before the launch. Consequently, although there was an air of secrecy about the event, there was clearly little security risk involved.

We waited in the main reception area, anxious to make our way beyond the oak-panelled doors to see what was awaiting us in the studio beyond. Presently we were ushered into a conference room, where we were greeted by Rover's

Right: *At Station Five, the front and rear suspension units are installed. Here the large stainless steel silencer and single-leaf rear spring are visible. Note the torque control arm, which is just visible, linking the axle to the forward spring mounting. (David Knowles)*

Below: *The RV8 bodies are suspended on specially adapted slings, salvaged from the former Cowley South works, where they were once used for the Rover 800. The axle table, visible just to the left of the bottom of the staircase, was salvaged from the Maestro/Montego production line. Note also the crates containing pre-assembled front suspension units, ready for bolting into the car. (David Knowles)*

Right: *The front suspension unit in place. This unit is brought in from outside the facility and includes sophisticated ventilated disc brakes and 'Goldline' suspension bearings. The basic front cross-member is a specially adapted MGB unit which, like a number of bodyshell components, is pressed at British Motor Heritage's Faringdon production facility. (David Knowles)*

Top: *Each RV8 engine comes pre-assembled from the Rover engine facility at Solihull in a special cradle, and is complete with the Rover 77mm gearbox already attached. Note the reference to 'Rover Adder' on the frame of the cradle. (David Knowles)*

Above: *Installation of the engine and transmission is a delicate operation requiring two men above and one beneath. The Cowley team manage to make the process look considerably easier than it actually is. (David Knowles)*

Below: *The finished car, fresh from the final manufacturing station, prior to emissions and safety testing, road testing and final valeting before despatch. (David Knowles)*

External Affairs Team of Michael Kennedy, Denis Chick, and Kevin Jones, together with the head of Rover Special Products, Steve Schlemmer. From there, we moved into the studio, where an intriguing MG-like silhouette, wrapped in a grey cover, had been positioned tantalisingly just visible behind a large screen in the centre of the floor. To one side of it was the full-size styling buck of the EX-E concept car which had first appeared at the 1985 Frankfurt Show and which looked as stunning as ever. At Michael Kennedy's invitation, MG Car Club Vice-President Bill Wallis and Roche Bentley of the MG Owners' Club ceremoniously unveiled the car, revealing the RV8 to us for the first time.

The Rover people were clearly keen to gauge our reactions to the new MG (a similar exercise had been carried out in 1982 prior to the launch of the MG Metro), and they were not disappointed. Even though there were mixed feelings about an MG sports car costing over £25,000, the basic formula of mating the MGB body to the Rover V8 engine was, by general agreement, a virtual guarantee of success. In fact, a few provisional orders for the car had been placed almost within minutes of its unveiling.

On Press Day, at the RV8's official debut in Birmingham, a few specially-invited MG enthusiasts and personalities (including Don Hayter) gathered round a massive white-walled turntable at the heart of the Rover stand. Once again, the basic MGB proportions were all-but unmistakeable beneath the dark-green cloth covering, but even to those of us who had been privileged to see the car the previous month, the air of anticipation was almost tangible.

Late in the morning, John Towers, Rover Group Managing Director, took his place on the rostrum and made a brief speech reflecting on the successful growth of the company and the significance of the car we were about to be shown. Then, without further ado, the cover was removed and the RV8, resplendent in the optional Le Mans Green Pearlescent finish, was there for everyone to see.

Despite the presence of strong attractions elsewhere, including the McLaren F1 car, there was a general consensus among those in attendance that the RV8 was probably the star of the Show — a judgment confirmed by the number of people who thronged around the Rover stand during the following two weeks. All that remained was to see how the motoring press and the car-buying public would react.

Press Reaction to the RV8

The response to the RV8 by the motoring press, who are inevitably a much more hardened and objective bunch of people than the majority of single-marque enthusiasts, was perhaps predictable. Rover had made a point of emphasising that the new car was not intended to compete for sales with other cars and not surprisingly the press latched on to that argument and turned it on its head. Its obvious rival was the TVR Chimaera, similar to the RV8 in terms of size, engine (Rover V8) and price, but featuring a reinforced plastic body and far more sophisticated suspension.

Unaffected by the octagonal bias of the average MG enthusiast, magazines such as *Autocar & Motor* and *Performance Car* were in two minds about the new MG. They were happy enough with its performance and thought that it managed effectively to overcome its comparatively primitive suspension; both, however, concluded that, for those not utterly smitten with the MG name, the TVR was a more rational purchase.

The Hillclimbing RV8

The launch of the RV8 soon led a few adventurous souls into considering its possibilities in motorsport. Among them was Dave Peers, of Rover Special Products, who had been responsible for the car's brakes, wheels, tyres, suspension and steering. Peers had also been involved with the MGB, when plans had been mooted for putting the O-Series engine in that car, and had contributed to the design of a well-known aftermarket coil-over shock absorber front suspension conversion for the MGB, which had led to Rover Special Products asking him to join them. He also had some 30 years' hillclimbing experience, so it was not surprising that he should favour this very 'gentlemanly' form of competition as the way to go. The opportunity to put this idea into practice arose when Peers noticed a green development car — the same car as was used for the RV8 brochure photographs — sitting neglected outside the offices at Rover's Gaydon testing and development facility. According to RSP's Mike O'Hara, the car was due to be pensioned off and ultimately scrapped, as are nearly all development vehicles. Then, in Peers' words, 'I said — Why not let me take it up the hills? — to which the reply was — That's a good idea!' Given the large number of relatively well-off enthusiasts who competed or spectated at events, and

who might be potential buyers of an RV8, hillclimbing was in Rover's eyes an ideal way of promoting it.

Prepared by Peers, the car has two drivers: Kim Johnson, who is manager of Paint Processes at Longbridge, with 20 years of racing MG Midgets behind him (shades of Bob Neville!); and Tim King, a former Austin apprentice who no longer works for Rover and who lives in Huddersfield. Whilst the RV8's engine is kept totally standard (but devoid of catalysts), a degree of work has gone into the drive-train and suspension. The car has been lowered by 2.5in, with stiffened and lowered springs and dampers. At the rear, a Panhard rod has been added to further improve axle location (the car already had anti-tramp bars) and further work has been carried out on the braking system. While the RV8 was being developed, two rear axle ratios were available for the GKN axle, with Quaife torque-bias differential. The ratio adopted for road cars was 3.31:1, which gives a relaxed 28.1mph per 1000rpm; the other was 3.77:1 and this was the choice for the hillclimbing RV8. Further changing the gearing, the tyres were changed from the standard 65 profiles to 50 percent aspect ratios, though the RV8's wheels were retained to keep the car looking as standard as possible. The overall effect was to lower the gearing by about 30 percent.

The interior was changed relatively little, other than the fitting of a roll-cage (not mandatory but fitted by Peers in the interests of driver safety) and the substitution of a bucket driver's seat for the standard item.

Thus equipped, the car debuted at the famous Prescott Hillclimb in July 1993 (pictured), where it attracted wide attention and acquitted itself honourably. Outings at Loton Park, Harewood, Curborough and Ragley Hall completed the 1993 season. Its schedule for 1994 includes plans to enter it in the 'Roadgoing Sports Car Class', which requires that cars should be run on road tyres only.

Photo: Derek Hibbert

Many people expressed disappointment that the RV8 seemed more of an expensive nostalgia trip than an all-new low-cost sports car in the spirit of past MGs. But this was missing the point: the MG RV8 had been defined from the outset as a limited edition car (which the TVR clearly was not) and as a car which, while deliberately invoking the original MGB, had cured many of its shortcomings.

In the first full road test of the RV8, on June the 16th 1993, *Autocar & Motor* commented favourably on the build-quality of their Nightfire Red specimen, K12 MGR, and approved of the high standard of interior trim, a world apart from that of the original V8. They were not so impressed with a 0-60mph time of 6.9 seconds, but enthused over the engine as '...far stronger in the mid range than screaming at the 5900rpm rev limit, so the technique is to change up early and let the torque do the work. Drive like this and the engine's flexibility becomes a joy, dispatching every 20mph increment between 20 and 80mph in fourth in less than 5.6 seconds.'

Although *Autocar & Motor* were clearly disappointed with many of the dynamic characteristics of the RV8, they admitted to finding it attractive: 'To us the RV8 is an anachronism, albeit a strangely likeable one'. In the same issue, a comparison test

with the Chimaera came out in favour of the faster (158 mph) and more accelerative (0-60mph in 5.2 seconds) TVR.

What Car? tested the same car as their weekly sister publication and also compared it with the Chimaera. Although concluding that the TVR was in many ways a more competent car, they were astute enough to recognise that mere excellence is not always the deciding factor, declaring that 'Those with a spare £25,440 who wish to rekindle happy MG memories of the '60s and '70s will get huge enjoyment from the proud new wearer of the famous badge.'

Performance Car tested the RV8 — K12 MGR again — in convoy with the TVR Chimaera, a Morgan Plus 8, a Ginetta G33 and a Marcos Mantara, in their August 1993 issue. The obvious link between these cars was the use in all of them of the same basic 3.9-litre Land Rover-built V8 unit, though the TVR unit produced 240bhp as against the 190bhp of the standard unit found in the remainder. John Barker led the *Performance Car* team on a three-hour rainswept journey from the Millbrook test track to Clwyd and was gratified to have chosen the RV8 as his vehicle: 'cruising the M6, heater breathing hot air into the leathery interior, the V8 ambling along at a restful 2700rpm, I knew I'd made the right choice.'

Left: *Second time around: the RV8 on display at the 1993 Motor Show. (David Knowles)*

When it came to assessing overall performance, however, the testers were in no doubt that the TVR was the car to beat and that the MG's 'traditional handling' was hard-placed to compete dynamically. 'Even so, the MG is a pleasant car to tour around in, with well laid-out and weighted controls, plump and supportive leather seats, excellent brakes and a sense of solid build quality. Stepping into the MG after the TVR lets you know just what an old design lurks beneath the smoothed-out, almost Bentley-like lines, but while the cockpit is narrow and lacks the appealing, generous curves and sweeps of the Chimaera's, it's a good place to be on a sunny afternoon.'

John Clelland, also in the *Performance Car* team, preferred the TVR but, like Barker, was clearly impressed by the RV8 too: 'My first thought on the MG was that a 10 year-old design couldn't be considered a serious contender, but I was to be proved wrong. Although not the best handling of the five, it was the quietest, smoothest and most effortless ride of all.'

British Cars magazine elected to pit the RV8 (K12 MGR again) against a Triumph TR8, postulating that '...if the chips had fallen the other way in the 'eighties, we could have been toasting the success of the Triumph RV8.' The magazine tested the RV8 alongside a 'state of the art' tuned TR8, rather than one of the (rare) factory originals, arguing that it would represent a better idea of the how the Triumph might have evolved had it been given the chance. Both cars were impressive, the magazine concluded, but they would appeal to rather different people, if only because the TR8 was a 'converted' car. The Triumph would be more likely to sell to a younger person who liked the styling, or to someone who has '...concluded that [the TR8] is one of the few metal-bodied V8s around to be had at a reasonable price.' Contrastingly, the RV8 was more of a GT car than an out-and-out sports car: 'It's plush, it's comfortable, it's got the right lines, it's traditionally British with the right heritage, but above all, it's exclusive.'

The Future

The appearance of the RV8 has inevitably prompted MG enthusiasts to ask the question, 'What next?' Understandably Rover have at this early stage given away little information about their forthcoming mid-engined MG sports car — codenamed PR3 — and no information at all about the prospect of other new cars beyond it. Nevertheless, some important facts have emerged. The first and most significant to RV8 owners

is that the current specification car is the only one planned: unless a dramatic change of policy occurs, there will be no 'Series II' RV8s with different equipment, altered body styles or larger engines, even though such changes are all technically feasible. Similarly, there are absolutely no plans to produce any left-hand-drive version, for the simple reason that the low volumes involved would not justify the expenditure.

Not that the RV8 is a home-market-only car. Following its launch in Japan, at the October 1993 Tokyo Motor Show, Rover's Japanese subsidiary received around 1,300 serious enquiries for the car. The changes needed were minimal: both the Land Rover Discovery and the Range Rover were already being sold in Japan, making any alterations to (for example) vehicle emissions specifications comparatively easy. Consequently, the first RV8s have already been shipped to Japan — complete with air-conditioning — with a smaller quantity allocated to Germany.

Aside from the need to comply with changes in legislation in the domestic market, which are not presently expected, it is planned to keep the car in production as it is for around two and a half years, by which time about two thousand will have been built. And that will be it: there are no plans to extend production beyond that quota, thus guaranteeing the exclusivity of the RV8.

Now that Rover have expended such resources of time, energy and money in producing the RV8, it does not require much intelligence to realise that, once again, MG appears to have an exciting future. Whilst the all-new PR3 small sports car, due in 1995, will take on such lower-priced competitors as the Mazda MX-5 and Toyota MR2, the RV8 will surely have paved the way for a new flagship MG sports car to challenge the best that Europe and Japan can offer — powered, perhaps, by a further evolution of that remarkable V8 engine.

Whatever the future might bring, we can surely hope that the RV8 marks the first stage in a renaissance of the MG marque which will be totally unlike the half-hearted revival attempted by the old Austin Rover management in the early 1980s; and it is likely that some of the styling features developed for the RV8 may well be reflected in future MGs. Whilst visiting the factory to see the first finished pre-production RV8, it was made clear to the author that if he could have passed beyond the large secured doors on one side of the studio, he would have seen things of more than passing interest to MG devotees. For the time being, however, 'the other side of the door' must keep its secrets...

7

MGB GT V8
— Maintaining The Breed

Buying an MG V8 — by Dave Wellings

Buying a decent V8 has never been that easy. For a start, the majority of those on offer will have been clocked: it is inconceivable that a car now close to 20 years old could still have much less than 100,000 miles on the clock, unless it is a quite exceptional vehicle. These cars were used as normal everyday transport, or certainly were until the factory closed in 1980, which was the catalyst sparking the level of interest we see today. Early examples would have been up to 70,000 miles by then, and even the latest V8s would have seen four years' hard use and covered something over 40,000 miles. A nominal mileage per year since 1980 would not in itself cause significant deterioration, but the condition of many supposedly low-recorded-mileage V8s available for sale suggests a considerably more-than-nominal mileage: the vast majority are in poor overall condition, despite a high asking price, and any prospective buyer should consider the cost of major refurbishment before paying over the odds for a V8 needing work.

So, if you wish to buy a V8, what should you be looking for? Fortunately, most V8 conversions are roadsters, and therefore there is little risk of finding a bogus factory V8 GT. Many converted cars have been described by vendors as 'Costello V8s': the name has an undeniable cachet, and a genuine example is appropriately higher in value. The buyer *must* satisfy himself that the car is indeed what the seller claims it to be, though the availability of parts with the Costello name on them does not always make this easy. The best procedure is to try to ascertain the known history of the car and, if possible, to check details such as carburettor installations, engine bay modifications and other structural changes against a genuine Costello.

The risk therefore is mainly that of a stolen car, or a re-shell, if it is important to you that the car in question is a genuine unre-shelled factory car. In most cases, some history can be obtained from the Register — if you have the chassis number. The original chassis plates were all reverse stamped, with raised characters, but replacement plates are invariably stamped with indented characters because of the difficulties in reproducing the original reverse stamping.

The body plate is the most difficult to reproduce. It is found in a shallow oblong indentation on the nearside of the bonnet shut panel. If this panel is replaced, the indentation is present on the new panel (and new bodyshells), but the steel strip which is stamped with the number is not. Since the shut panel rarely rots out, this is a good indication of a likely front end shunt, or a new shell.

Right: Dave Wellings, V8 Register Technical Representative, provides words of wisdom on buying a V8. (David Knowles)

Recognising a genuine original shell is somthing of a challenge. The rubber-bumper shells are the same as the equivalent 1800cc 'B GT, especially from the 1976 facelift on, when the 1800cc car was fitted with a single electric fan and had the radiator moved forward to the V8 position. So the body number is really all you have to go on. The V8 shell was usually, though not invariably, prefixed G75D. The chrome-bumper V8 shell is more distinctive from its smaller-engined contemporary than is the case with the later cars; under the bonnet, the inner wings (similar to those of the rubber-bumper cars) feature prominent 'dishing', essential to provide ade- quate clearance with the V8 lump installed.

The oil cooler is behind the grille, above the lower front panel, not suspended below it as in the rubber-bumper specification. On the bulkhead where the steering column passes through, no securing bolts or captive nuts should be visible, since the column is secured in two locations under the dash. The rubber-bumper shell has a single three bolt under-dash fixing, and is secured to the bulkhead by three bolts with captive nuts, visible under the bonnet.

Under the rear wings there are two bolt heads, easily visible on each side. These are the rear damper mounting bolts. On the chrome-bumper shell, all four stand proud of the panel. On the later rubber-bumper shell, the front pair are recessed into the panel, (possibly for tyre clearance). All Heritage shells are to the later specification in this area. The chrome-bumper shell has two countersunk Phillips setscrews at the forward edge of each front footwell, with nuts visible under the car. Rubber-bumper shells do not appear to have this feature, which is of indeterminate purpose. Creating a convincing chrome-bumper V8 bodyshell from either a contemporary

Left: This is the nearside inner wing of David Knowles' V8 during restoration and after grit blasting, showing how serious the rust in this outwardly fairly sound car had become. Corrosion in unrestored, poorly restored or neglected V8's is typically this bad or even worse. (David Knowles)

Left: The most critical structural components of the MGB GT V8 are, as with all MGBs, the sills. This is a view of the inside sill step of David Knowles' V8 during stripping out for restoration; these holes were all hidden by the rubber sill covering and the footwell side trim panels. Note the holes at the forward end of the footwell sides, which are seen to more effect from the other side in the previous photograph. (David Knowles)

1800cc shell, or from a Heritage shell, is not straightforward, but it is certainly not impossible.

The condition of the bodyshell is crucial, since a significant part of the cost of the restoration will be spent in getting the shell right, even if you do it yourself. If you have to pay someone else, then the price, if you want it done properly, can be prohibitive. Off-the-shelf panels do not just bolt on, and it is unrealistic to expect them to. The front wings are often a compromise, and fit badly at the leading edge. Generally they are a bit too long and fit badly round the grille — particularly important on chrome-bumper cars.

Original wings when stripped of paint generally exhibit significant body solder around the leading edges which shows the amount of hand-finishing required when the bodies were built at Pressed Steel and why the wings fitted comparatively well in this area. Without this attention, not only will there be a poor fit between the wings and grille, but the common solution of fitting the bonnet as far forward as it will go to line up with the leading edges of the slightly overlong wings results in a large gap between the scuttle and the bonnet.

The rubber seal which sits in the scuttle channel is worth examining for overspray, since it is rarely replaced, and seldom masked. Also check the bonnet/wing gaps. Invariably, replacement wings will display a gap which is wide at the extremities but which narrows midway — particularly noticeable when viewed from the front. Another indicator of replacement wings can be found at the rear top corner, adjacent to the 'A'

post. On original wings, as the door-shut flange approaches the 'A' post, it gently tapers away. Reproduction wings do not generally have this taper. On rubber-bumper cars, the ill-fitting front edges of the front wings are less obtrusive, since the bumper masks most of the imperfection.

Replica Honeycombe grilles are of variable quality, and unless you are familiar with the real thing, are not always easy to identify. The original alloy surround was very easily damaged by flying stones, and was apt to tarnish quickly. The chromed surrounds of the reproduction grilles are more resistant to denting, and should last well. Note that the plastic Honeycomb is 'handed' on original grilles — the diagonals running one way protrude further than the diagonals running the other, and the halves of the grille mirror each other. Reproduction Honeycombs often have the protruding diagonal the same on each side.

Doors can present a major problem, since genuine replacement doors are blessed with variable amounts of twist along their vertical axis. Around the quarterlight fixings on the top edge of the skin are a number of spot welds, and if these are drilled out, the skin can be twisted slightly on the frame; this may be enough to make all the difference in fit. Remember to re-weld the skin to the frame!

The striker plate and hinge adjustment are crucial. It may even be necessary to remove the captive blocks from within the door and shave off some metal to get that last fraction of an inch adjustment. If all else fails, the hinges can be taken off and reshaped. This is all time well spent, and the fit of the doors will to some extent reflect the quality of a rebuild. The quarterlight itself is fully adjustable for height, by the insertion of shims, (factory shims are pieces of plastic), and the amount of 'lean' can be set up using the five fixings. The rear glass runner is adjustable for 'lean', and for 'fore and aft' movement, and the upward limit of window travel is adjustable, so that a satisfactory door fit should, with patience, be achievable.

Don't rule out a car purely on the basis of badly fitting doors: with some effort, a major improvement can be effected. The simplest way to identify a replacement door is to examine the leading edge of the frame. Doors after 1976 have a small circular hole through which the speaker wires pass; earlier doors did not have this hole. Re-skinned doors can usually be identified by the quality of the flange-work, or in some cases by a peculiar profile round the door-lock.

On the sills, the seam with the front wing should be unfilled and should match exactly with the leading edge of the door. The rear seam should be body-sealed, but visible. Reproduction sills will tend to result in an over-wide seam at one end, and some will have oddly-shaped drain-holes. Beware the short cover-sill: this is a short term bodge covering the visible outer sill between the wings, and cars so fitted should be avoided. At the base of the 'A' post, examine the horizontal flange where the bottom of the post meets the sill. It is difficult to get this right, and many cars are seam-welded at this joint. Stainless cover-sills are now on the retreat: treat them all with suspicion.

Rear wings are best fitted complete, but this is the most expensive option and not always necessary. If the tailgate overlaps the 'C' posts, then the rear wings are fitted too close together.

The tailgate itself is surprisingly difficult to fit, especially with new seals. When fitting it on to a newly painted shell, there is a major risk of damaging the paintwork. The upper tailgate seal is another useful indicator of a respray, being so difficult to remove or mask that it often shows overspray. Additionally,

KEEPING THE GREAT MARQUES ALIVE

One of the most respected marques ever known, the familiar MG Octagon is still proudly displayed on classic cars the world over. Along with the already familiar Austin Healey Sprite, these cars continue to capture the imagination, just as Moss Europe continues to supply the parts to keep the spirit alive.

In the UK alone, Moss Europe employs over 120 people engaged in technical ... resourcing discontinued lines, answering customer queries and ensuring that only ... ect parts for your particular model of classic car are supplied.

... arts catalogues are held in high esteem by both amateur and professional vehicle ... s alike. Comprehensive, yet clearly written, each catalogue is only £2.50 including ... provides the most up-to-date information available. With a publication to cover ... hicle in the range of MG, and Triumph sportscars, Moss leads the way in model-literature.

... the six UK Moss branches is a Heritage Approved Specialist. Run by enthusiasts, ... aintains the same commitment and personal service to MG, Triumph and Austin

Healey owners of all ages - yet Moss parts remain competitively priced and easily accessible.

With over 24,000 different lines available, Moss is proud to be the largest and most comprehensive specialist parts supplier in However, Moss still maintains a close relationship with all of its customers -

especially through innovative schemes such as personal customer cards to ensure swift and accurate ordering, and Moss Motoring newsletters. Whatever your specific parts requirement, speak to Moss Europe first. No one knows more about your classic car. For more information, contact your local branch outlet or call Moss Europe's Customer Service Department on 081 948 8888, or fax on 081 940 0484.

adjustment at the hinges is very restricted. The fit of the tailgate seal to the lip around the opening must be exact to eliminate both fumes and noise. It can be reshaped with care to achieve this. Rattles can usually be eradicated by adjusting the catch, either up and down, using the two bolts, or in and out with carefully applied force. Examine the lower halves of each rear wing. Most repair panel joins will be visible from the inside by examination of the vertical panel behind each rear wheel.

Beware the lower half panel fitted over the top of the corroded original; the giveaway is the wheelarch lip, which will either display two edges or be exceptionally thick. (Don't confuse this with the normal join between the inner and outer panel.) Additionally, look for obvious filler around the seam where the wing meets the sill, and around the rear lamp cluster. Welds may be visible inside the wing at the same level as the waist strip on the outside; if the repair panel is correctly fitted, there will be a joddled joint at this level. The lack of a visible join here, coupled with the indicators noted above, almost certainly confirms the double rear wing bodge. There may also be a curiously flared arch effect, best viewed when looking down the side of the car. Properly fitted lower half repair panels are notoriously difficult to get right, due to the double curvature, and the long weld which is necessary.

On the rear panel, early cars had a leaded seam vertically through the filler neck aperture, and at a corresponding place on the nearside. On later cars, this join is outboard of the filler neck, and visible: thus the later panel is wider than the early panel. This change may have taken place just before the change to rubber bumpers, but in the majority of cases the rule is that the seam is *not* visible on chrome-bumper cars but *is* visible on rubber-bumper cars, despite what you may have read elsewhere!

With the advent of rubber bumpers came a further modification, with the welding of three reinforcement plates to the lower section of the panel. Each of these plates is identical but selectively drilled, according to location. The panel joints at the top of the 'A' posts, and 'C' posts also became 'unleaded' and visible around the facelift of 1976, that of the 'C' post being covered by the GT flash introduced at that time. A careful scrutiny of the brightwork should reveal whether or not these items are original, or to original specification, since reproduction chrome bumpers have strangely contoured ends which are 'cut off' and, in many cases, the bolt holes don't line up, making the fit uneven. Overriders are generally good, but beware the reproduction rubber buffer — the reproductions display a sharp vertical crease down the length, resembling the keel of a boat, whereas the originals are gently rounded.

Reproduction waist mouldings are usually very poor, and badly rippled. Do not confuse them with original mouldings which have been badly fitted. They are very problematical to fit, and it is all-too easy to finish up with a dent over each wing fixing. They are also 'handed', so check that the angled ends match the panel edges! The BL badge on the front nearside wing should have an indented motif; the reproductions have the logo 'printed' on a flat foil plate.

Wheels are easily available — at a price. Some of the new ones have indifferent chrome, and the backs of the alloy centres of the new wheels understandably lack the 'Dunlop' and the date markings. The new casting is also much sharper on the back than the original. The valve should fall between two cut-outs on the wheel centre, and point squarely up a black 'spoke'. When the wheels are reconditioned, they may be reassembled incorrectly, resulting in the valve being offset from its proper position. A reconditioned centre will also display erosion of the pattern; after two rebuilds, the raised alloy circle is likely to merge with the adjacent raised surrounds to the cut-outs.

The other problem with regard to wheels is that progessive batches of replacement centres are losing their shape (presumably as the tooling wears out). The tapered end is disappearing, as is the recess where the centre badge sits. The original 175HR14 tyres are becoming increasingly difficult to source, with the result that 185/70s and 195/70s are now commonly fitted. Even the smaller of these is a tight fit in the boot space. Early V8s had the split boot floor which is hinged a few inches from the seat-back, whereas later cars have the one-piece boot floor. Consider the 195/70HR14 as the maximum realistic fitment to the standard car since wider profiles will probably foul the wheel arches, and 60 series profile or less will do nothing for the ride or handling.

Interiors changed little during the V8's production run. Colours offered were Navy, Ochre, Black and Autumn Leaf. The tunnel, front footwells and rear-seat base panel were carpeted, and the rest of the floor pan had rubber mats. Some very late V8s seem to have had conflicting colours, such as Black tunnel carpet with Autumn Leaf floor mats and Black sill mats. This may have been to use up the stock of rubber mats prior to the change to full carpeting in 1976 — which the V8 never got, of course. In conversation, former Chief Body Engineer Jim O'Neill stated: 'Colour charts for production use were issued by the Design Department. If there was a shortage of any component, it was recorded on the Build Card and a large 'Shortage' label was attached to the windscreen. In the case of any shortage, Production were not allowed to deviate from the approved specification without a concession or deviation note issued by the Chief Engineer. I certainly would not have authorised a mis-match of colours, but that is not to say that it didn't happen!'

Early press photos show the speedometer on the right and the tachometer on the left. This was reversed, probably for all production cars.

The dual oil pressure/water temperature gauge was unique to the V8, but at least two different types were fitted. Early cars had twin needles which rested parallel at nine o'clock, while in later cars the temperature needle rested at the eight o'clock position. Some cars may have been fitted with the 1800cc gauge. Both the choke knob and bonnet release knob changed from 'round' to 'T' handles, and the heater control knobs changed from small to large.

Nor, during the V8's production history, were there many significant changes under the bonnet. The workshop manual shows a rubber sleeve on the choke cable, but this does not seem to have been adopted for production. Twin fans were standard, of course, and essential. A manual override switch for the fans is a worthwhile and popular modification. A pulley guard was fitted to the radiator header tank for the first few hundred cars, before being discontinued. The early radiator was secured by six bolts, three each side, and with side-brackets which were angled top and bottom. Later radiators have four fixing bolts, two each side, with squared-off side-brackets. The oil pressure take-off was originally from the remote filter head, but was later moved to the oil-pump baseplate. At the changeover, some cars had a blanking plug fitted to the filter head, but subsequent castings were not drilled for the take-off.

The electrical relays on the inner offside wing remained consistent for most of the production run, though some of

Right: *Derek and Merie Sharman judging a rubber-bumper MGB GT V8 at the keenly-fought Concours during the MG Car Club's premier May Bank Holiday Silverstone International Weekend, 1992. (David Knowles)*

the last V8s had the later round plastic relays fitted.

To recognise the 'correct' engine installation, examine the front cover. There should be a two-bolt blanking-plate low on the nearside, where the manual fuel pump fitted on the Rover P5/6 saloon installation. SD1 front covers have the same basic casting shape but it is not opened up. Check also that the original engine number casting (nearside, next to the exhaust downpipe) has been sawn off and that the number appears on the block, at the rear of the nearside cylinder head, adjacent to the bell-housing.

The Land Rover front cover will also fit, and is used on the RV8, but is obvious since the water pump is much higher than original. If tubular manifolds are fitted, the inner wings must be dressed to allow adequate clearance. The sump should have a centre well, and be shallow front and rear. This is to clear the cross-member (front) and the exhaust cross-pipe (rear). The SD1 sump does not have the rear relief and so the exhaust must be mounted lower to clear.

Check around the back of the air collector box and make sure that the crankcase breather and filter are present. Also check that the carburettor overflow pipes are present, that they join at the 'T' piece and locate on the drain tube attached to the bellhousing. Examine the fuel pipe between the carburettors — it is often bodged, in which case you should fit an armoured length of proper petrol pipe. You must remove at least one carburettor to do it, but don't use short cuts or your car may go up in flames one day. Heat build-up in the relatively confined engine bay of an MGB V8 is always a problem, so any measures which can be taken to minimise it most definitely should be taken. Check that the starter motor heat-shield is there; if it isn't, make one up and consider making it larger than the standard item. Most owners will have experienced the clicking solenoid effect at some time and I can only put this down to heat sink into the motor when really hot, so a modification here may help.

Finally, apply all the usual used car checks to your intended purchase. Don't set aside your commonsense and buy the first car you see just because it's a V8: there are plenty of them around, so be patient and be prepared to travel. If you take your time and apply all the essential criteria, you will be rewarded with a truly classic MG; if you choose badly, you will have ample time in which to regret it! And beware of the classic car speculator masquerading as a private vendor. There are still some about!

Concours — by Dave Wellings

Anyone familiar with concours, and especially those who have taken part in them, will be aware of just how widely judging standards can vary. The owner of an MGB V8 will find that at one event the judges know very little about the car, while at the next he will be faced with judges who know 'too much' and will heavily penalise his V8 for what seem the most trivial reasons. It must always be borne in mind that judging, even when the most unambiguous criteria are in force, is often a highly subjective activity. However, when you think you ought to have won but haven't, there is one simple rule of thumb to apply: would you exchange your car for the winner's? If you would, then there are no grounds for complaint!

So what are the judges looking for? Externally, the paint-work and brightwork must be as near perfection as it is possible to get: external changes to the V8 were few, so there is little scope for controversy. The same applies to the underside (finished at the Pressed Steel factory in body colour, though perhaps not as thoroughly as it should have been): few changes, so few causes for argument. The exhaust on the V8 differs from chrome- to rubber-bumper examples and early cars had a drain-plug in the petrol tank; but these are about the only significant differences.

Interior changes, too, are all fairly obvious. The mixed-colour floor coverings on late V8s might provoke some interesting discussions with judges, but by and large interiors are well documented and consistent.

The main area of contention lies under the bonnet. It would be quite unrealistic to assume that the entire production run had identical fittings and this is where entrant and judge may have differing opinions. V8 guru Geoff Allen has confirmed that the factory used whatever was available at the time, but can provide the following guidelines:

Above: *The engine of John Heagren's multi-award-winning MGB GT V8 was rebuilt by Robbie Shaerf of LV Engineering, based in West Hampstead, London. (R. Shaerf)*

- Underbonnet soundproofing varied in type

- Most, but not all, V8s had turquoise throttle cables

- In most cases, the throttle-cable was *not* attached to the bracket on the pedal-box, despite the fact that photographs in some sales literature may suggest otherwise.

- Sundry clips and fasteners varied in colour and type.

- The location and quantity of adhesive labels varied.

- There were at least three variations of radiator: 1) with pulley guard; 2) with angled side-bracket and six fixings; 3) with square side-brackets and four fixings.

- Air-filter boxes should have a very fine hammered finish and the sponges should be a light creamy beige colour.

- The only badges ever fitted to the sides of the front wings were a single square 'BL' badge and a 'V8' badge on the nearside wing only. There were no badges at all on the offside wing, though many owners fitted them subsequently.

John Heagren, Concours Champion

John Heagren's V8 is well-known throughout the concours world, for not only has he achieved the highest awards possible amongst his peers, but he has gone on to challenge and defeat all comers in the hotly-contested world of the classic car concours masterclass — including the coveted National Benson & Hedges Award. As he recounts below, John is unusual in having owned his car from brand-new.

'In the autumn of 1975 a good friend of mine witnessed a V8 being delivered on a transporter to a British Leyland dealer. He contacted me immediately, as he knew that I was interested in owning one. I viewed the car within an hour, while it was still on the transporter; I subsequently put down a deposit, and a week later I was the proud owner of a Flamenco Red MGB GT V8.

'My intention was to keep the car for two or three years and then sell it, but after attending my first MG Club event, in 1976, I changed my mind. There were many MGs with their bonnets up, displaying their immaculate engine bays, and I noticed that the majority of them were in far from original condition. Many parts in the engine bay were chromed, and I also couldn't help noticing that various non-standard components such as Wolfrace wheels had been fitted. Paintwork, too, was often non-standard. I felt that my car looked extremely dull in such company!

'That winter I spent a lot of time and effort transforming my car. I put on a set of Wolfrace wheels and a front 'air dam' spoiler. I chromed various engine bay components and added extra V8 badges. In the context of the time I felt that the car looked great, and it gave me great confidence when attending shows.

'Over the next ten years I was successful at many events, but as the car was non-standard I found that I was limited with regard to the shows I could enter. The top prizes were the concours ones, so I decided to convert the car back to original again. This of course involved the fitting of the original Dunlop V8 wheels and the original front valance, as well as reverting the engine bay to standard and removing the extra V8 badges!

'An uncompromising eye for detail and cleanliness is all-important if you want a successful concours cars; the difference between coming first and second often hinges on the minutest points. I have been involved in classic car competitions for over seventeen years now, and for the past five or so I have been active in judging concours cars; it's a task which I thoroughly enjoy and through which I have gained a great deal of knowledge of a very wide range of marques and models.'

MAJOR AWARDS:
51 Premier Wins; 7 Master Class Wins;
41 Car of Show awards;
Benson & Hedges International Champion, 1989;
Best MG in UK, at NEC, 1990;
over 350 trophies won to date.

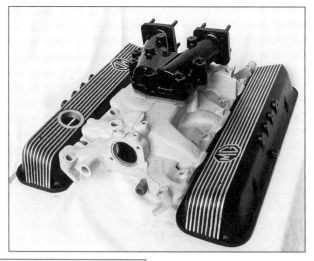

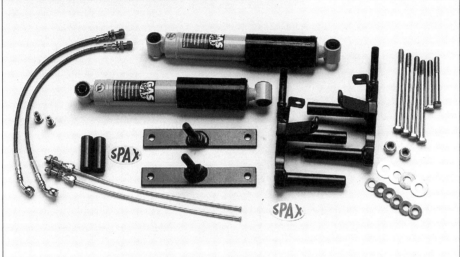

Above left: Ron Hopkinson of Derby offers this conversion for the front suspension of any MGB, which cleverly dispenses with the original lever arm shock-absorber by replacing it by a conventional (and easy to replace) telescopic unit.
(Ron Hopkinson)

Above: As well as instigating the remanufacture of the unique MGB GT V8 rocker covers, with their integrally cast MG logos, Clive Wheatley also offers the special inlet manifold arrangement unique to that car.
(Clive Wheatley)

Above: One of a number of products aimed at improving the standard MGB suspension which are produced by MOSS, this kit is a budget shock-absorber conversion which includes new brake pipes. (MOSS Europe)

Below: One of the more enterprising 'MG people' is Clive Wheatley, seen here posing alongside his own MGB V8 roadster and advertising the specially fabricated Janspeed exhausts which he sells to order. (David Knowles)

Other non-standard parts such as manifolds, carburettors, front cover, gearbox, thermostat-housing etc should be obvious and therefore unlikely to be disputed.

It will, of course, be greatly to the concours entrant's advantage if he has found out everything possible about his car's 'personal' history and is able to produce documented evidence of its conforming with original specification. And don't be discouraged if your car doesn't finish among the winners: concours are all part of the learning process and, win or lose, are a great way to meet fellow-enthusiasts.

The Specialists

Maintaining an MGB GT V8 — or indeed almost any classic car — simply would not be possible without the existence of a wide network of spares and services organisations. In former years, owners had to rely either on new car dealers (whose interest dropped in direct proportion to the age of the vehicle concerned), a smattering of car factors which tried to cater for many different marques and models, or the chance of finding what they wanted in one of the numerous scrapyards throughout the country. The emergence of the classic car movement, which really only got under way in the early 1970s, led to the growth of a specialist industry geared towards individual marques and even particular models, drawing expertise largely from enthusiastic owners and restorers but also from disillusioned former new car part distributors.

For the MGB V8 owner, there are in Britain what may be regarded as three tiers of specialists: the relatively big companies, such as MOSS, M&G International, Ron Hopkinson and Brown & Gammons, who are able to use their resources to fund and develop tooling for obsolete components; the middle range of companies, such as the V8 Conversion Company and Beer of Houghton, who often tend to limit themselves to fewer models or offer a more specialised service; and the smaller companies, frequently one-man bands, such as Geoff Allen, Clive Wheatley and Peter Burgess, who provide a personal level of service and/or unique products which the larger companies cannot or will not offer.

The following is not intended to be an exhaustive directory of specialists — there are simply too many companies around for that to be feasible — but it will provide the V8 owner with a guide to the services which he is most likely at one time or another to require.

Above: This picture shows the lengths restorers may have to go to in order to eradicate rust from a V8. This car has received complete new sills and is seen here in the midst of having the rear wings replaced. (David Knowles)

Below: Peter Berry fabricated this engine-hoist to facilitate engine removal. Note the correct angle of repose of the suspended engine/transmission unit which simplifies removal and installation considerably. (Peter Berry)

Right: The impressive headquarters of the MG Owners Club in Swavesey, near Cambridge. (Richard Monk)

The Large MG Specialists. There are two companies in particular which dominate the MG parts-specialist scene; both advertise widely in the motoring press, produce high-quality catalogues, and issue regular and informative newsletters. The companies in question are **MOSS Europe**, an outer-London based affiliate of the North American company of the same name, and **M&G International**, who are situated in the north west and have built up a similarly high reputation. In 1993 the two companies came together when Ingham PLC, owners of M&G International, acquired MOSS Europe; the two still trade as separate outlets, but their research and development teams now work in collaboration to avoid duplication of effort with re-tooling and bulk buying.

MOSS Europe are well-known for their extensive coverage of the MG and Triumph sports car scene, having grown from beginnings as the merger of the Sprite & Midget Centre and Cox & Buckles. Along the way, a number of reputable experts have climbed aboard, including the V8 Register's own Spares Representative, Peter Beadle. Peter is responsible for researching and developing new parts for MG owners, and has to his credit a number of hitherto unobtainable parts which help to keep our cars on the road. MOSS do not confine themselves to the business of supplying parts for old cars as museum pieces or fine-weather-only classics; they have recognised that many people still use their MGs as everyday cars and have developed improved components such as more up-to-date trim and sophisticated suspension upgrades. This involvement in improving the breed rather than just addressing the status quo has been extended to their involvement in motorsport where, in conjunction with Penrite Oils, they are generous sponsors of the MG Car Club's top-ranking BCV8 Championship.

Amongst the particularly interesting products the company can provide is a coil-over-shock-absorber kit, which allows the front end of the MGB to be upgraded to similar standards to those of the new RV8. Although this conversion is not cheap, it is undoubtedly the most sophisticated kit available and a most useful improvement for the higher mileage MG motorist.

M&G International are no less active in the sporting arena, sponsoring the MG Owners Club Racing Championship and offering a range of products and services to rival those of MOSS. M&G regularly offer some of the best price reductions in the business, backed by an efficient despatch service.

Ron Hopkinson, based at Derby, offers a full range of competitively priced parts for the MG V8, but is best known, perhaps, for its well-developed — and again sensibly priced — suspension-handling kits. Developed by Harvey Bailley, the famous suspension consultants, these kits are among a number of unique products in the Hopkinson catalogue. The Ron Hopkinson telescopic damper conversion kit for the MGB front suspension is a popular seller, and utilises a conventional full-size damper unit. The company are also keen to point out that their handling kits include seven-eighths-inch front and five-eighths-inch rear anti-roll bars, which are the same sizes as adopted for the RV8.

Brown & Gammons are renowned for their expertise in both the restoration and racing of MGs: both Ron and Malcolm Gammons have built up enviable competition records in classic car events, showing the world how competitive the MGA and MGB can be, given the right preparation. Ron Gammons is particularly proud of the export success of his company: 'Some 80 percent of our business is in parts sales, of which we stock some 16,000 lines, and over 40 percent of those sales are overseas.'

Also into this category falls the mammoth **MG Owners Club**, which furnishes an extensive range of spare parts, accessories, servicing and restoration facilities from their recently-built Cambridgeshire headquarters. The club uses its considerable size to good effect in negotiating bulk discounts, which are then passed on to members in the form of discounted spares for a range of models, including the V8. An extensive accessory range for these cars is also offered and is featured in an impressive Accessory Catalogue.

The Mid-Size Specialists. For the owner who wants something a little different, **Mike Satur** of Great Houghton, near Barnsley, offers a highly respected trimming and restoration service including full re-trims in Connolly leather and exquisitely-crafted walnut dashboards. Mike is a long standing member of the V8 Register and can offer many services of specific interest to MG V8 owners.

One specialist who has a long association with the MG marque is **Beer of Houghton**, based in Cambridgeshire. The Beer family has MG blood in its veins, Syd Beer owning probably the most comprehensive collection of MGs outside any museum (including the former *Motor* road test car, HOH 933L) whilst his son Malcolm sweeps all before him in the MG Car Club/MOSS BCV8 Championship. The Beer family is renowned for its particular expertise on the MGB GT V8, which extends to full rebuilds to road or race specification.

Another specialist heavily involved with the fitting of V8 engines into MGBs is Dave Vale, of the **V8 Conversion Company**. Dave has specialised in V8 conversions for many years and has produced an invaluable handbook for would-be converters, which includes dimensional sketches.

The Smaller Specialists. The number of MG concerns falling into this category are almost infinite; we limit ourselves here to those particularly relevant to V8 owners.

One of the first specialists to cater for the MGB GT V8 was David Franklin of the **Huntsman Garage** in Bristol, among whose many notable achievements was the building of Terry Smith's successful V8 racer. **Geoff Allen**, whose recollections appear earlier in this book, used to work at the MG factory and has a virtually unrivalled position as one of the most knowledgeable MG service and restoration experts in the business. At his modest premises in Abingdon, Geoff has serviced, rebuilt and converted more MGs than he cares to remember. The high standard of his work is confirmed by the fact that he is invariably booked up months in advance. Clearly enthusiasts find the wait worthwhile.

V8 Register Committee member **Clive Wheatley** has been successful in getting parts remanufactured where others have failed — for example, the distinctive MGB GT V8 cast aluminium alloy rocker covers, the chrome-bumper V8 grille badge plinth (remade in alloy rather than the original poor quality plastic) — and he has even uncovered the whereabouts of the original British Leyland wing badge tooling. Currently Clive is investigating the possibility of getting a batch of the original (and unobtainable) cast-iron MGB GT V8 exhaust manifolds cast.

As with most other power units, cylinder head modication plays a vital role in the tuning of the V8 engine. One of the foremost experts in this field is **Peter Burgess**, who not only offers exchange cylinder-heads but also undertakes the rebuilding of customers' own engines.

8

MG V8 Conversions — by Roger Parker

This chapter describes some of the routes and options most often encountered in V8 conversions. It is not intended as a complete 'how-to-do-it' guide, and those who require more detail are advised to contact the V8 Register.

Conversions of the MGB, either roadster or GT, to V8 power can be divided into three categories, which are listed here in *descending* order of difficulty:

- ✦ Three-synchromesh gearbox Mk1 cars (1962-1968)

- ✦ Four-synchromesh gearbox Mk2 cars (1968-1974)

- ✦ Rubber-bumper cars (1974-1980)

By far the easiest cars to convert are those with the late rubber-bumper type shells, as by that stage the chassis and in particular the engine bay had been rationalised with that of the V8. Converting one of these cars to V8 power is largely a bolt-in operation — provided that factory parts are used throughout. The detail work can of course vary considerably and will depend upon the desired end-result. Fuel injection, for example, will clearly necessitate many additional alterations to the fuel and electrical systems.

The work involved in converting an early MGB to V8 power is considerable, since the early three-synchromesh gearbox cars had a narrower transmission tunnel and, in the case of the roadster, a different back axle for which suitable ratios are unavailable. The gearbox is similarly unsuited to adaptation to the V8 engine. To convert such a car will therefore necessitate the replacement of many components and will involve significant alteration to the body, especially since the majority of early MGBs are more likely these days to have been painstakingly restored to their original specification.

The following guide serves as the basis for all conversions.

Three-Synchromesh Cars

Body. The early MGBs were fitted with a gearbox basically the same as the MGA's, the external dimensions of which are considerably less than the later four-synchromesh gearbox and much less still than the Rover SD1 gearbox favoured in many conversions. To fit a standard MGB V8 gearbox would require widening the gearbox tunnel, whilst to fit the SD1 gearbox would necessitate raising the roof of the tunnel. Note also that the larger 9.5-in clutch of the V8 (MG or Rover)

Above: Roger Righini of Lausanne, Switzerland owns this MGB V8 roadster, which he built from the basis of a 1977 US-specification MGB. Fitted with an engine from Brown & Gammons and a Rover SD1 five-speed gearbox, the car achieved first in class at the 1988 MGCC Silverstone International Concours. (Roger Righini)

requires a larger clutch housing, and thus only the later rubber-bumper cars will not require alterations to the gearbox tunnel in this area.

Although the V8 engine will fit neatly in the MGB engine bay, there are some critical components and significant tight spots which will need alteration, specifically the engine mountings, the rear compartment bulkhead and the inner wings. The later rubber-bumper cars and any genuine factory V8s provide the ideal pattern for the alterations required.

Engine Mountings. The four-bolt square engine mounting plates welded to the chassis rails will have to be removed and either the later rubber-bumper type plates (round, with a single bolt) or appropriate after-market conversion parts fitted; the former are fortunately still available. The fitting position is virtually the same, but the exact measurements should be obtained by examining a late rubber-bumper car. After-market mountings rely upon the dimensions quoted by the supplier, and as such are more variable. This can of course lead to other dimensions being out and consequently other parts being more difficult to fit. As a general rule the after-market mountings leave the engine sitting higher than is the case for the rubber-bumper type. The choice of mounting will therefore have considerable influence on sump clearance, induction system to bonnet clearance, and even tunnel modifications.

Roger Parker

Roger Parker is well-known in MG circles, particularly for his involvement in both MGB V8 conversions and tuning the MG Maestro. He owns a V8 roadster and a rare MG Maestro Turbo and writes authoritatively about both in the two club journals, *Safety Fast!* and *Enjoying MG*. He was also deeply involved in the well-publicised John Hill Twin-Cam MGB and his own MG Maestro Twin-Cam, both of which were fitted with a modern two-litre Rover M16 engine.

As a motorway patrolman on the M6 in the West Midlands, he has found that MG ownership usually brings out the best in motorists… which is not to say that possession of an MG Car Club membership card will be of any benefit to traffic offenders!

Roger built his first MGB V8 transplant in 1985, using an MGB GT body and a Rover SD1 engine which was uprated and fitted with fuel injection. A second car, utilising an early MGB roadster bodyshell, followed in 1987.

In July 1989, David Bishop of British Motor Heritage asked Roger to bring his V8 roadster to Rover's Canley plant, to which at the same time Bishop and a colleague brought the first Heritage-bodied MGB (TAX 192G, known for obvious reasons as 'TAXI') and the last MGB roadster, both from the Heritage Collection. The purpose of the gathering was to show the cars to about a dozen top-level Rover management personnel, who were investigating the possibility of Rover's building a new MG sports car.

After the meeting, the party moved to an internal factory road where all three cars were lined up. Roger continues the story: 'There was a reasonable degree of interest from most, especially those who recalled their younger days when the MGB was really something special. Interest was heightened by a look under the bonnet of my car, particularly the fuel injection and the fact that all the parts were from the Rover stable. Next, someone asked if he could take a drive around the factory, a request which I readily granted. The remaining members of the group were assembled in twos and threes and were chatting among themselves until the engine was fired up. Then conversation stopped — not due to excessive noise but because of that distinctive V8 burble. Another fellow jumped into the passenger seat and they were off and away.

'Witnessing my own car being driven off was an unusual experience for me, and I have to say that both sight and sound gave me immense pleasure. When it returned a few minutes later, both occupants emerged with ear-to-ear grins; comments such as 'superb' were passed, followed by requests from others to have a go. All, without exception, pronounced themselves most favourably impressed by the car, its performance, handling and braking. There followed a close examination of the engine installation and the fuel injection system, questions such as 'How could we do this today?', and discussions about means of complying with legislation. By the time the meeting was over, nostalgia had given way to an enthusiastic debate about the viability of producing a new MGB with a specification similar to my own.'

Roger is modest about his car — 'I'd be the first to admit that it's hardly show condition and wouldn't win any prizes'. Understandably, though, he is proud of the small part it may have played in the decision-making process which led to the birth of the RV8.

Inner Wings. On the inner wings of V8-engined and late rubber-bumper cars, near the engine mountings, are two indentations which provide clearance for the exhaust manifolds and hot air pick-up. (Terry Mitchell recalls that these indentations were actually designed by Tony Felmingham to introduce stiffness into an otherwise flat panel; they were known at the factory as 'Felmingham's Follies'.) With the variance in engine mounting position and after-market exhaust manifold kits, some will require this extra clearance and some will not. The ones that do need the additional clearance are normally the more efficient, since the curvature of the primary pipes is to a larger radius, and so it may be necessary to modify the inner wing area accordingly.

Radiator Mountings. The radiator in any four-cylinder cars prior to the 1977 model year facelift is set well back in the engine compartment, and is consequently wrongly positioned to suit the longer V8 engine. The existing radiator mounting plate and flanges should be removed and the later rubber-bumper-type fixing should be welded in place, using dimensions taken from a later car.

Oil Cooler Platform. The oil cooler mounting panel and supporting box underneath will also require alteration. As these two panels fit between the chassis rails, the easiest solution is to remove both of them completely and replace them with the appropriate rubber-bumper panels, which will provide all the necessary holes and mountings for the under-slung oil cooler as fitted to those cars. Alternatively, if the original panels are to be retained, then both have to be cut back towards the front of the car to the same dimensions as the rubber-bumper cars, with a new closing panel specially fabricated to restore rigidity. In this manner the oil cooler will be retained on top but it will have to be moved forward and to the right, under the bonnet lock platform, as per the chrome-bumper factory V8.

In addition, this option will require new captive nuts and the need to discard the normal 13-row oil cooler, which will be too tall to fit. A 10-row cooler, as fitted to factory MGB GT V8s, will fit into the available space with ease. It should be noted that retention of the original oil cooler, whilst an obvious attraction from the point of view of economy, would probably over-cool the oil on a pure road car.

Remote Oil Filter Head Mounting. The oil cooler on standard Rover V8 engines is mounted on the lower offside of the engine, in a location which would clash with the front cross-member in an MGB. When the factory produced the MGB GT V8, they relocated the oil filter on a remote fitting fixed to the offside inner wing, just behind the radiator mounting plate. It follows that a V8 conversion will require a similar installation and this can use standard MGB GT V8 oil hoses, which are still freely available. The mounting flange required is an 'L'-shaped bracket which fits between the offside radiator mounting plate and the inner wing. It is a good idea to utilise a flange similar to the factory car's, since this will align the filter head pipe inlet (from the oil cooler) with the appropriate access hole through the radiator mounting plate. Note that any fabricated mounting flange must be sufficiently rigid to resist the twisting force required to remove a tight oil filter.

Gearbox Tunnel. If the Rover SD1 five-speed gearbox is to be fitted, various other factors need to be considered. The SD1 gearbox will require a longer propshaft with a consequent greater arc of propshaft movement; in addition, after-market propshafts are usually of larger diameter than the original, and this further adds to the space problems. A common problem resulting from this is lack of clearance at the curved reinforcing panel which ties the rear inner sides of the two floor panels together; this may need to be removed and replaced by the more deeply curved rubber-bumper item.

Four-Synchromesh Chrome-Bumper Cars

Modification of these cars follows the basic guidelines covered above in the section on three-synchromesh cars, with the exceptions detailed below. For reference, this category includes all post-1968 Mk2 cars, i.e. GHN/D4 and GHN/D5 cars up to the end of chrome-bumper MGB production.

Body. The only significant difference to be considered here is the much larger tunnel area on these later cars. The gearbox is basically the same type as fitted to the factory V8 and if the standard V8 gearbox is being used, no changes should be necessary. To fit a Rover SD1 gearbox, it will be necessary to raise the height of the forward area of the gearbox tunnel to that found at the rear of the tunnel. (Note: these comments assume the engine is to be mounted to the same dimensions as the original factory V8. Any variation from this *will* have a knock-on effect on other body modifications and this should be taken into account.)

Other body modifications are exactly as per those described for the three-synchromesh cars.

Rubber-Bumper Cars (Post-1974)

Pre-1977 four cylinder cars retained the original radiator location and fixings, although the remainder of the engine compartment was similar to the factory V8 set-up, and therefore no bulkhead or inner wing alterations will be required. If the Rover SD1 gearbox is to be fitted, the tunnel clearance will need to be modified as already described, but apart from that the installation is far simpler than with any other bodyshells. The only problem, for those who wish to produce a chrome-bumper car, will be the removal of the reinforcements used to mount the rubber bumpers and to reinstate the small curved area beneath the rear light clusters, together with the use of chrome-bumper front wings and front valance instead of the rubber bumper units; fortunately the latter are mostly bolt-on replacements.

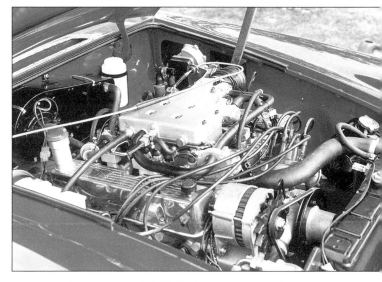

Above: Phil Guymer's superb 'MGB V8 EFi' features early Federal/Australian-specification Rover SD1 Lucas electronic fuel injection, allowing a normal bonnet line. (Roger Parker)

Below left: Current-specification Land Rover hot wire fuel injection system laid out prior to modification and fitting to Roger Parker's MGB V8 EFi. (Roger Parker)

Below: Peter Burgess produces these 'Econotune' Rover SD1 heads which are worth between 25 and 40bhp on a 3528cc V8, depending on remaining engine and ancillary specifications. (Roger Parker)

Top: This was the last MGB roadster to be converted to full V8 specification when brand new by the V8 Conversion Company of Farnborough, Kent. The engine is a Rover P6 unit with a 10.5:1 compression ratio, mated with a lightened flywheel and transmitting power to the road via lowered suspension. Ventilated front discs were added by owner Peter Gee of Eynsford, Kent. (Peter Gee)

Above: Steve Holder decided he would have an MGB GT V8 with a difference, and the result was this purposeful metallic BRG 'MGC Sebring' lookalike. Note the double bonnet-bulge (based on an MGC pattern) which was necessary to clear the centrally mounted Rover SU carburettors. (Roger Parker)

Below: There will surely not be many MG V8s like this one built by John Hill's MGB Centre in Redditch. Seen here at Land Rover's Solihull premises in the autumn of 1992, it was built to promote the company and is based on a Range Rover chassis. (Roger Parker)

The Heritage Bodyshell

If the donor bodyshell is badly corroded, and requiring significant repairs in addition to any necessary structural alterations, serious consideration should be given to using a British Motor Heritage bodyshell, which has the obvious advantages of structural integrity and superior corrosion resistance. Since both chrome- and rubber-bumper Heritage shells are available, a further decision will have to be taken. The rubber-bumper shell will require little work other than cosmetic alterations (if a chrome bumper car is the desired result), whereas the chrome-bumper shell will necessitate alterations in the engine bay as already described. On the down side, the rubber-bumper shell will raise the rear suspension pick up points by one inch, which does nothing for the handling.

Reducing this unwanted height can be accomplished by using lowered springs. Do remember, though, that the springs need to be able to locate the rear axle and transmit the torque of the V8 engine, so that correct selection is vital. The front ride height was, of course, also raised by a similar amount, but this was accomplished by the use of a modified cross-member rather than by any structural bodyshell changes, giving a little more leeway with regard to deciding the chosen method of lowering; this is covered in more detail in the sections on steering and suspension.

Steering (Pre-Rubber-Bumper Cars)

The modifications already described will allow the V8 engine to be fitted along with either the MG or SD1 gearbox. We have also looked at the necessary alterations to the cooling and oil systems. However, these alterations alone would result in the original steering column fouling the offside exhaust manifold, in addition to which the bulkhead alterations will have removed the steering column lower mounting. There are several solutions to this problem. The early Costello cars, and a number of more recent conversions, use a modified steering column and pinion shaft in which the originals are shortened and then rejoined using a length of shaft with two universal joints.

The factory solution, and the one which I favour, is to use the V8/rubber-bumper MGB steering rack assembly along with the corresponding column assembly. This will of course necessitate the fabrication of suitable brackets to suit the mountings required. As these later column units are much bulkier collapsible types, it follows that the original aperture between the speedometer and tachometer will not be wide enough to accommodate them, and so the later 80mm dials and cowling will be needed.

These alterations alone, however, will be insufficient, since the type of cross-member will have a significant effect on the rack mounting. If an original chrome-bumper unit is to be retained, fitting the later rack will cause the pinion shaft to point towards the clutch master cylinder, rather than the hole in the bulk-head. This will necessitate realignment of the rack mountings on the cross member to pull the pinion shaft into the correct position. Careful alignment of the pinion shaft with the column is vital in order to achieve the correct steering operation and feel. If the rubber bumper cross-member is used then the rack will line up correctly but you will then have to deal with a raised suspension! From this, you will have deduced that the steering is not going to be sorted out cheaply, as virtually the whole system has to be changed or modified.

Above: Among the more ferocious beasts to be found in the USA is this MGB fitted with an Oldsmobile turbocharged V8 unit. Developed from the Buick original, the Oldsmobile featured modified cylinder heads with superior combustion chambers. (Tom Studer)

Any solution will involve considerable work and expense, to an extent which even so-called 'experts' fail to anticipate.

New V8/later rubber-bumper steering racks are available with no exchange and there are also a few later new columns available. And you could always use RV8 components as these are to the same basic pattern as late rubber-bumper parts.

Steering (Rubber-Bumper Cars)

This section could not be simpler, as the rubber-bumper cars all used a steering set-up the same as that in the V8s.

Suspension (All Cars)

How one deals with the suspension will be determined by whether the car in question is a chrome- or rubber-bumper example. With the chrome-bumper bodyshell, ride height will pose no problems; on the rubber-bumper cars, it was increased by adding an extension to the front cross-member and lowering the spring pick-up points on the rear of the body. The simplest way of lowering the suspension on rubber-bumper cars is to utilise lower springs. If further lowering is required, it must be taken into account that the steering geometry will be altered significantly (this is true even if lower springs are used), probably with a detrimental effect on handling. The only practicable solution to this is to utilise a chrome-bumper front cross-member: this would lower the suspension pick-up points and retain normal suspension geometry — but it is important to appreciate that the steering rack and pinion angles would then have to be altered to suit (see section on steering). Don't forget the problems of engine mounting, either.

Detail specifications will depend entirely upon individual preferences and must be given serious consideration. For example, the suspension kits now available do work and may certainly be considered a worthwhile addition. However, when changing the car to V8 power a further and highly important consideration is the location of the rear axle, which is liable to move under torque and consequently affect the car's handling. It is recommended that axle anti-tramp bars should be fitted, which will have the side-benefit of allowing the rear springs to be softer than would otherwise be the case. Without anti-tramp bars, genuine V8 or MGC springs should be employed and this in turn will mean stiffer front springs to

achieve a proper balance. My own V8 roadster uses MGC roadster rear springs with standard MGB GT (or V8) front springs; with the original roadster front springs, the front was found to be too soft.

In addition to choice of springs, it is important to decide which dampers (shock absorbers) should be used. Standard lever arm dampers when in good condition are well-suited to the car, particularly when fitted with uprated valves; but they are prone to early leakage, leading many owners to prefer telescopic dampers. For many years there have been telescopic damper kits available for the MGB's rear suspension; these are quality components and well worth acquiring although, when they are adjustable, too many owners adjust them too hard and therefore reduce the damper to little more than a semi-solid link between the axle and the body. In these conditions the body rolls very little, giving a false impression of improved handling. More recently, a number of conversions for the front suspension have appeared, with varying degrees of success. By far the most effective are those which replace the front damper completely, substituting a fabricated link and separate telescopic damper — which must of course be properly balanced in relationship to the rear set-up.

The simplest route to improved handling is to use the standard lever arm damper set-up, perhaps with the uprate valves fitted and the addition of one of the anti-roll bar kits. Taking matters any further than this will necessitate the use of both front and rear kits from one specialist alone, to avoid any imbalance between incompatible set-ups.

The last point to consider when dealing with the suspension is the state of the rubber bushes. Those in front should be the V8 'metalastic' type, whilst the remainder should be standard ones in good condition. Harder (for which read solid!) competition bushes are available, but provide a bone-jarring ride which is inappropriate for normal road use. Note that rear suspension bushes will have a reduced life when coping with V8 torque and will therefore require more frequent replacement. Additional rear axle location, by means of anti-tramp bars, as discussed, will reduce this wear to some extent.

Brakes (All Cars)

Compared with other aspects of V8 conversions, brakes are relatively easy. As a minimum requirement, you should aim to imitate the factory MG V8 set-up, which uses a slightly thicker disc than the standard MGB and different callipers. The MGB GT V8 pads have a greater friction area, resulting in improved efficiency.

Today there are a number of vented brake disc kits available, with either two- or four-pot calipers, at prices from around £330 upwards. Most of these use discs of about 9.5in diameter, as against the 10.75in of the factory V8 solid discs. You may find that the improvements in the vented discs are offset to some extent by the reduced diameter, giving very little overall improvement for the considerable investment required.

The MG RV8 uses a 10.6in-diameter vented disc with a four-pot caliper and these parts are available through normal Rover spares outlets. Fitting them to an MGB will certainly be possible... but only if the whole of the front suspension is changed. Fitting of individual RV8 parts may also be possible, but is not yet known.

Many conversions have retained the original MGB brakes but fitted with competition linings (as in the original Costello cars), such as the Mintex 171 range of pads. These will work

well enough for normal driving, but (and it is a big but!) there will not be much in reserve to cope with heavier use. Cars not fitted with a servo are few and far between (other than the early cars), but it must be appreciated that the purpose of a servo is to reduce the amount of pedal effort needed when operating the brakes, not to increase braking efficiency.

Rear brakes fitted to the factory V8 were basically stock MGB roadster items (not GT), with the smaller bore cylinders preventing premature lock-up. The friction linings were different, but in practice normal MGB items will suffice if balanced with the use of V8 front brakes. Remember that braking is normally split 80 percent front and 20 percent rear.

Above: The latest and most sophisticated Costello conversion to date is this beautifully finished British Racing Green car which features Costello's own fuel injection layout, the Costello five-speed gearbox and very effectively uprated brakes. Compare the discreet Costello badge (right) with the original version shown in Chapter Three. (Roger Parker)

Wheels and Tyres (All Cars)

Standard MGB wheels are satisfactory, although perhaps a little too skinny for the V8. A minimum of 185 section width tyres with appropriate profile ratio should be acceptable — eg 185/70-HR14. Standard wire wheels are definitely out of the question; uprated 72-spoke wire wheels are adequate (from personal experience), but will suffer from the effects of V8 torque in the long term.

Alloy wheels are the obvious and sensible choice, with up to 6in rim width being possible inside the standard rear wheel arches, depending upon tyre choice and the retension of the standard wheel offset. a 5.5in or 6in rim with a 195/60 tyre (ideally V-rated) provides a good all-round compromise.

The standard MGB SR-rated tyres will not only be not up to the job but will also be illegal, as such tyres are only rated for speeds up to 113mph.

Transmission (All Cars)

Whichever gearbox is selected, the 9.5in standard clutch will cope with power levels up to around 250/260bhp and probably more, since the MGB is not a heavy car. The choice of gearbox is wider than might be first assumed. The most commonly chosen is the Rover SD1 'box which is widely available in the UK and relatively cheap. Fitting involves modifying the rear gearbox mountings, obtaining a longer modified propshaft (with ends to suit gearbox and axle). The speedometer cable then has to have the SD1-type gearbox end fitted to it using an overdrive-type MGB cable long enough for the job. Lastly the SD1 clutch slave cylinder needs to be mated to the MGB master cylinder via an appropriate flexible pipe.

The second choice is a genuine MGB GT V8 gearbox, which will usually fit with minimal modifications. The propshaft will be virtually identical to the original, the same in length but with bigger flanges, like the SD1 gearbox. There are, however, a couple of drawbacks: firstly, the gearbox is rare and correspondingly expensive; secondly, it had a reputation for being distinctly marginal under MGB GT V8 torque!

Third choice is the standard MGB gearbox fitted via an adapter plate, and as this already physically fits it is an attractively economic proposition. However, if the V8 gearbox is marginal, the standard MGB 'box is even less suitable and cannot be recommended.

The Costello five-speed gearbox has been designed specifically to suit the V8 engine and the MGB four synchromesh

Above: *Engine bay of the new Costello car. Note the smart 'Costello' injection plenum chamber which allows the standard MGB bonnet to be retained. (Roger Parker)*

models without the need for any modifcations. Personal experience has proved this gearbox to be extremely strong, with superb ratios, its only weakness being a change quality which can be baulky. Cost is reasonable at around £900, with no exchange.

Finally there is the Getrag gearbox, as fitted to the racing Rover 3500 Vitesse in that car's heyday. Having used these gearboxes in Jaguars over very high mileages, I have been unable to fault them. (Top MGB racers also use this set-up.) Costs and the problems of locating a suitable bell-housing will probably prevent many from choosing the Getrag. Additionally, a special propshaft would have to be fabricated.

Also to be taken into consideration is the rear axle and final drive ratio. The V8 needs a taller gearing ratio and the 3.07:1 crown wheel and pinion set provides the ideal ratio. Retention of the standard MGB ratio of 3.9:1 in fact renders the first gear virtually useless. The rare 3.3:1 and 3.7:1 CW&Ps can be used to good effect, though the 3.7 is still slightly low-geared.

The Choice of V8 Engine

Any of the Rover V8 engine series can be used, but the units from Rover saloons are undoubtedly the best. Range Rover, Land Rover and Sherpa versions employ the larger Range Rover-specification water pump which uses a different front cover, and although the cover can be changed or the water pump modified, it is easier to choose a saloon engine in the first place. It is also advisable to choose a later engine. From 1967 to 1973 a rope type rear oil seal was fitted which can cause problems at high mileage and is impossible to get at without removing the engine. In 1973, this was replaced by a superior lip seal — as used on the MG V8 engines.

In 1976 the SD1 was launched and with it came numerous improvements to the engine, specifically the oil system, ignition system and cylinder heads. Developments after 1982 included fuel injection, improved block casting and of course larger capacities — 3.9, 4.2 and soon 4.5 litres. The source of the engine will determine what particular 'bits' are required. A Rover P6 (2000 shape) will provide the correct crank and water pump pulleys. If it is an early model, it will also provide

the correct 'top loading' alternator mount and adjustment link. Such an engine will have the correct front cover assembly, but will not provide the uprated oil pump and easy facility to fit the later electronic distributors. Conversion is possible, but not straightforward.

The SD1 unit is the ideal base engine, on to which the front pulleys and alternator mount from a Rover P6 3500 should be fitted. Use of a Range Rover engine would necessitate in addition to those parts an appropriate front cover assembly.

Induction Systems (All Cars)

A variety of induction systems can be fitted, but only a few will fit under the standard MGB bonnet. The standard MGB GT V8 inlet manifold extension, with rear mounted twin SU carburettors, is now available again and is both reasonably priced and satisfyingly competent. Its use will involve machining down a standard SD1 manifold to accept the extension.

A most popular conversion is the fitting of a Holley carburettor on an Offenhauser manifold which with a low rider air filter just clears the standard bonnet. Setting up can be a problem as specialists with the necessary knowledge and experience of these systems are by no means commonplace. On balance, the twin SU option is simpler and less liable to tuning problems. Either option will work well with the normal MGB fuel pump, provided it is in good order. If the Holley option is chosen, then the 390cfm model is the one to go for: anything larger will increase noise, reduce low-end power and waste fuel.

A recent addition to the market is a 4 SU crossover system, rather like some of the multiple Weber competition arrangements. It is claimed that this set-up offers greater mid-range power, and in theory top-end power should also be good. The age-old problem, though, is the overall height, which once again will be similar to the original Rover SUs.

Fuel injection might be described as the 'Rolls-Royce' option, but it will make the conversion a great deal more complicated. Bonnet clearance is the main problem, with the two basic options being to machine the normal Rover injection manifolding to suit or to fabricate a suitable bonnet bulge. It would be sensible to acquire a complete system from an SD1 or a Range Rover, as individual components will prove expensive. Machining an injection manifold is a task which should be undertaken only by those who *really* know how to do it. One option is to use a pre-1989 Airflow Meter system and replace the manifolding with the USA Federal/Australian-specification SD1 manifold. But even this set-up will necessitate up to one inch being machined off to fit under a standard bonnet. A further alternative is to use the later Hot Wire system (same as in the RV8) and machine small amounts of both the inlet manifold and the ram stack assembly where they join, thus providing the extra clearance needed to clear the standard MGB bonnet.

A fuel injection set-up will also involve a number of other alterations, including a separate extra wiring loom, usually sourced with the injection system. Fitting this will be quite simple, as it can be separated from the original loom except for five connections. Other changes involve a modified fuel tank or extra swirl pot, high-pressure fuel pump (eg the commonplace Bosch system) and both feed and return fuel lines.

Whatever induction system is used, a cold air pick-up is a good idea, as MGB underbonnet temperatures often get high enough to vaporize fuel.

Exhaust Systems (All Cars)

A very simple area to cover, since the multitude of tubular manifolds available all follow virtually the same pattern. Cost and quality are the main criteria, with the smoothness of bends and clean internal tracts being the most important considerations. The main system can be whatever is desired, but most follow the original MG V8 pattern of a two-box single pipe. The standard system results in a quiet but deep 'whoofle' sound which is pleasant for cars in everyday use. Other systems have a much louder and 'sportier' sound, which might be regarded by neighbours as anti-social! As far as performance is concerned, the standard exhaust system will provide excellent results and will not prove restrictive until around 200bhp. Thereafter the system will become progressively more restrictive, and as an alternative a number of specialist systems are available, most of which have a bore of 2.5in instead of the original-equipment MGB GT V8 bore of 2.25in.

Stainless steel exhaust systems are considerably more expensive than the mild steel variety, and the choice really boils down to the type and amount of use the car is given. My own V8 roadster's mild steel system has lasted over six years.

Cooling Systems (All Cars)

H ere the easiest and most effective option is to imitate the standard MGB GT V8 system, together with the standard V8 hoses, which will make spares easier to find. The MGB GT V8 water pump is identical to that fitted to early Rover saloons and will fit front covers with the exception of Range Rover, Land Rover and Sherpa types. The radiator should be either the standard MGB GT V8 item, or the alternative higher-capacity item now available. Cooling fans should be electric and a manual over-ride is a highly sensible addition which is worth considering for original factory cars as well.

Oil System (All Cars)

A gain, this should imitate the factory V8. (The RV8 follows a similar pattern, except that its more efficient radiator eliminates the need for a separate oil cooler.) In the section on body modifications, reference was made to the underslung oil cooler, which should be the ten-row type to avoid over-cooling; this will also have the advantage that all the hoses and fittings can be acquired from any of the numerous parts specialists. Either the pump base or the remote filter head can be used to provide a take-off for the oil pressure gauge.

Electrical Systems (All Cars)

C hanges required to the electrical system will depend largely upon the age of the basic car and the type of induction. A three-synchromesh car will need to be changed from positive to negative earth, and this will cause many headaches with the necessary wholesale replacement or modification of many items such as the windscreen wiper motor, indicator flasher unit, radio (if fitted) etc. Various modifications to the original wiring loom will be necessary, if only because some of the components are located differently from in the original MGB, e.g. the coil and the distributor. Bearing in mind the fact that the wiring loom in the transplant car will probably have seen better days, it is well worth considering substituting an all-new item.

Above: Pictured at the Sheraton-West Port in St Louis, Missouri, this car is the result of a joint exercise by Robin Weatherall of the MG Centre in St Louis and Ken Costello. The fountain is not standard equipment! (Robin Weatherall)

Below: Engine bay of the same car, complete with Costello fuel injection and Costello five-speed gearbox. (Robin Weatherall)

The factory-built V8s were fitted with an AC Delco alternator and had their own starter motor with different electrical ends from the MGB. Early cars in particular will need to have their charging circuit wiring beefed up, as dynamo-type cars produce much lower current than those with the higher-output alternator. The standard MG V8 AC Delco unit puts out 45 amps — double the output of MGB dynamos — whilst the more freely available and arguably superior Lucas A127 type starts at 45 amps and rises to over 80 amps, in its more common versions. The tachometer will need to be recalibrated for eight cylinders or another gauge may be fitted.

Other Considerations

W ith the fitting of the much more powerful engine, several other improvements are worth considering. The headlights should be uprated to decent halogen units, perhaps supplemented by appropriate driving lamps. Inside, more supportive seats would be a good idea for leather-seated MGBs which, particularly when cornering at speed, leave a lot

Above: Don Hayter's smart Brooklands Green V8 roadster was built using an ex-development O-Series MGB bodyshell and incorporates many features which could have been used in production V8s. (Don Hayter)

to be desired! Finally, don't be tempted to skimp on the conversion: do a thorough job that you can be proud of. This will also work in your favour when obtaining insurance, as you will be able to show a complete and competent conversion which can be regarded as a safe proposition on public roads.

Costello Developments

Although he will always be remembered as the man who brought together the MG and the V8 engine, Ken Costello is still active today, even if not to the same extent as formerly. His current mainstream activity is the production of his own five-speed gearbox, which uses up much of his time but has not brought an end to the production of Costello V8s to special order. Ken's conversions have progressed significantly since the early days and offer a viable alternative to the enthusiast who does not want or cannot afford the new RV8.

The example chosen reveals the flexible parameters within which Costello conversions can be carried out. It is based on a very late, very low-mileage rubber-bumper GT, which has been completely stripped and rebuilt from the bare bodyshell. The aim in this particular case was to retain the anonymous look of a chrome-bumper car but to provide it with all the attributes found in a more modern car and with the performance and road-manners of a top-flight sporting model. Based on a 3.5-litre Range Rover unit, the engine has been enlarged to 4.2 litres and is fuelled by Lucas fuel injection, as is the RV8. Unlike the RV8, there is no need for a bulged bonnet.

The original Costello cars featured a bulged bonnet in order to clear the standard Rover SU carburettor. However, having engineered the bulge out of his later cars, Ken naturally felt that to revert to it in the current generation would be a retrograde step. He therefore designed and manufactured a new plenum chamber which, with a few minor modifications, fits to the standard inlet manifold.

The use of a Range Rover engine, which retained that vehicle's standard front pulleys, cover and water pump, also called for some subtle changes, which pre-empted the RV8 by a couple of years. Elsewhere the engine bay will be a familiar sight to V8 enthusiasts, parts and their positioning being little different from other versions.

Power and torque are transmitted through one of Costello's own five-speed 'boxes, which has more than enough capacity to cope with such prodigious outputs. The most significant feature of the design is that it will replace the original MGB four-synchro or MG V8 gearbox without any

need for body or mounting changes. The remainder of the transmission follows the MG V8 format, with the addition of a limited slip differential.

Suspension comprises a modified Ron Hopkinson kit along with front and rear anti-roll bars. The detail settings of the dampers are subtly altered and there are a couple of other suspension tweaks added. Wheels and tyres are the not-unfamiliar 'Minilite'-look alloys of 5.5Jx15, fitted with 185/65x15 'V' speed-rated Michelins.

Stopping this potent package are vented discs clamped by modified Vitesse four-pot callipers at the front and drums at the rear. These are controlled by a late 'B tandem master cylinder and direct servo. Close to the master cylinder and plumbed into the hydraulic circuits are two USA-sourced cherry-red canisters which are claimed to reduce the tendency to wheel lock under heavy braking, a sort of primitive ABS.

Inside, the rich smell of leather and the high-quality trim make an immediate impact. The use of dark leather does dim the interior, but it will survive better and with less maintenance than the RV8's light tan leather trim. Whilst the interior retains the original late-MGB pattern, it still looks right, and this is without the use of any burr walnut cappings. Another positive feature is the use of electric windows, which are so well-fitted and efficient that they seem to be original equipment.

Start the engine, and the subdued but purposeful exhaust note awakes a feeling of excited anticipation. Engage first and move away, and the ease with which the car is controlled is instantly noticeable.

Performance is stunning — on a par with that of the RV8, but with that indefinable extra 'punch'. The gearbox ratios are exactly right, with only a degree of baulkiness in the gear-change being a nuisance. But this small problem is quickly mastered, after which the car is pure delight. The suspension is compliant yet taut, resulting in sharp and responsive handling on smooth surfaces. On rougher roads, or when repairs are encountered in mid-corner, composure is upset to a small degree; however, it is still on a par with the RV8, which is itself considerably better than the original MGB.

Given the car's performance, it is of course necessary to ensure a much-improved braking ability. The car poses no problems in this respect, although due to the 25mm smaller front discs, there is not quite the reserve of braking as will be found in the RV8.

One specific design requirement for the car was that its owner should be able comfortably to cover high mileages in today's traffic conditions. The conversion achieves that goal by the updating of most areas to acceptable modern levels, if not beyond. Further, its non-aggressive styling is unlikely to attract the wrong kind of attention — another plus factor, given today's car-crime rates.

Overall, this beautifully finished MG achieves its aims of being both a 'classic' and a practical daily car for the 1990s. Its heritage will always show through, yet the updates are so effective that its owner is truly getting the best of both worlds.

In the meantime, as well as his work within the UK, Ken Costello has been involved in an exciting project involving the conversion of North American cars to 'lean green' V8 power. In partnership with Robin Weatherall of the MG Centre in St Louis, Missouri, a smart fuel-injected MGB V8 roadster has been built and has been shown during 1993 at various MG meetings across the country. American enthusiasts may be denied the RV8, but this new Costello conversion is surely an enticing alternative.

Appendices

MGB GT V8
and MG RV8

TECHNICAL SPECIFICATIONS

Feature	MGB GT V8		MG RV8	
ENGINE	Rover 3.5 Litre V8		Rover 3.9 Litre V8	
Location and Drive	In-line, front, rear wheel drive			
Capacity	3,528 c.c.		3,946 c.c.	
Number of Cylinders	eight			
Cylinder Layout	90 degree vee			
Bore (mm)	88.90		94.00	
Stroke (mm)	71.12		71.12	
Compression Ratio	8.25:1		9.35:1	
Cylinder Head	aluminium alloy			
Cylinder Block	aluminium alloy			
Valve Gear	single cam, two valves per cylinder			
Ignition	Lucas Distributor		breaker-less	
Fuel System	Twin SU HIF6 carburettors		Lucas multi-point fuel injection	
Maximum Power Output	137 BHP at 5,000 rpm		190 PS at 4,750 rpm	
Maximum Torque	193 lb.ft at 2,900 rpm		318 Nm at 3,200 rpm	
TRANSMISSION	4-speed all-synchromesh with reverse. Laycock overdrive operable on top only		LT 77 5-speed all-synchromesh with reverse	
	ratio	*mph/1000 rpm*	*ratio*	*mph/1000 rpm*
Fifth	(Overdrive) 0.82	28.50	0.79	28.97
Fourth	1.000	23.40	1.00	22.90
Third	1.259	18.59	1.40	16.40
Second	1.974	11.85	2.09	10.98
First	3.138	7.46	3.32	6.91
Final Drive Ratio	3.071 to 1		3.31 to 1	
STEERING	Rack and Pinion with collapsible steering column			
FRONT SUSPENSION	Independent with coil springs and lower wishbone mounted on cross-member assembly. Lever type dampers with double levers carry top end of swivel pin. Anti roll bar		Independent with double wishbones, coil springs and concentric telescopic dampers	
REAR SUSPENSION	Tube type live axle with three-quarter floating drive shafts. Semi-elliptic multiple-leaf springs. Lever type dampers		Tube type live axle with three-quarter floating drive shafts. Semi-elliptic taper-leaf springs. Telescopic dampers, twin lower torque control arms and anti-roll bar	
FRONT BRAKES	10.7 inch (272 mm) diameter solid discs		270mm (10.6") diameter ventilated discs	
REAR BRAKES	10 inch (254 mm) diameter drums		225mm (9") diameter drums	
SERVO	Servo-assisted Hydraulic			
WHEELS	14" x 5J composite alloy centre with steel rims		15" x 6J cast alloy	
TYRES	175 x 14 HR		205/65 x 15 VR	
DIMENSIONS				
Overall Length	154.75" (3,931 mm) Chrome Bumper 158.25" (4,020 mm) Rubber Bumper		4,010 mm	
Front Track	49" (1,245mm)		1,260 mm	
Rear Track	49.25" (1,251mm)		1,330 mm	
Wheelbase	91.125" (2,315mm)		2,330 mm	
Width	59.94" (1,522mm)		1,694 mm	
Height	49.96" (1,269mm) *		1,320 mm	
FUEL TANK	12 Gallons (54 Litres)		11.2 Gallons (51 Litres)	

* Footnote: The overall height of the V8 remained at 4 feet 1.96 inches (i.e. 49.96" or 1,269 mm) throughout production, although rubber bumper rear springs do have a different part number to those of chrome bumper cars (BHH1133 for chrome bumper; BHH1771 for rubber bumper). There was no justification or need to raise the suspension of the V8 in the manner of the four-cylinder cars because the V8 was not exported to North America. In contrast, the chrome bumper MGB GT (4-cylinder) was quoted as 4 feet 1.75 inches (1,264 mm), but this was increased in October 1974, with the adoption of the rubber bumpers, to 4 feet 3 inches (1,295 mm) an increase of 1.25 inches (32mm).

MGB GT V8 COLOURS AND TRIMS

Name	Number Built#	Paint Code	Current (Approx.)	Description	Navy	Ochre	Black	Autumn Leaf
					TRIM (Nylon Cord)			
					1973 only		1974/76	
ACONITE	100	BLVC 95	1974-1975	Purple				●
BLACK ❏	81	BK 1	1974-1976	Black			○	○
BLACK TULIP	5	BLVC 25	1973 only	Dark Purple		●		●
BLAZE	143	BLVC 16	1973-1975	Orange	●		●	
BRACKEN	155	BLVC 93	1973-1976	Light Orange/Olive				●
BRONZE YELLOW	26	BLVC 15	1973 only	Yellow Ochre	●			
BROOKLANDS GREEN	16	BLVC 169	1974-1976	Mid/dark Green				●
CHARTREUSE	19	BLVC 167	1975-1976	Pale Primrose			●	
CITRON	265	BLVC 73	1973-1974	Vivid Greenish Yellow			●	
DAMASK RED	471	BLVC 99	1973-1976	Maroon	●		●	
FLAMENCO RED	146	BLVC 133	1975-1976	Scarlet			●	
GLACIER WHITE	515	BLVC 59	1973-1976	Bluish White	●		■	■
GREEN MALLARD	15	BLVC 22	1973-1974	Dark Green		●		●
HARVEST GOLD	185	BLVC 19	1973-1974	Golden Beige	●		●	
LIMEFLOWER	2	BLVC 20	1973 only	Greenish Beige	●			
MIRAGE	17	BLVC 11	1974 only	Pale Grey			●	
POLICE WHITE	2	-	1973-1974	Off White	●		●	
SANDGLOW	9	BLVC 63	1975-1976	Sandy Beige				●
TAHITI BLUE	90	BLVC 65	1975-1976	Bright Mid-Blue			■	■
TEAL BLUE	244	BLVC 18	1973-1974	Mid Blue		●		●
TUNDRA	92	BLVC 94	1974-1976	Olive Green				●

MG RV8 COLOURS AND TRIMS

Name	Paint Code	VIN Code	Description	Stone Beige (Leather)
BLACK	BLVC 644	PMF	Black	●
BRITISH RACING GREEN	BLVC 617	HNA	Dark Green (M)	●
CARIBBEAN BLUE	BLVC 911	UME	Deep Sea Blue (P)	●
FLAME RED	BLVC 818	COF	Bright Scarlet	●
LE MANS GREEN ❏	BLVC 1202	HPD	Medium Green (P)	●
OLD ENGLISH WHITE ❏	BLVC 1205	NNX	Creamy White	●
OXFORD BLUE ❏	BLVC 1203	JSJ	Navy Blue (P)	●
NIGHTFIRE RED	BLVC 916	COQ	Wine Red (P)	●
WHITE GOLD	BLVC 933	GMK	Pale Gold (M)	●
WOODCOTE GREEN ❏	BLVC 1204	HPE	Olive Green (P)	●

Key:

M = Metallic finish; P = Pearlescent finish; ● = Standard Trim; ○ = Optional Trim Colour choice; ❏ = Optional Paint olour at Extra Cost; ■ = trim colour for Glacier White and Tahiti Blue could be Black or Autumn Leaf but this was not a formal option; # = Numbers of cars built in each colour supplied by V8 Register Historian Geoff Allen; **VIN** codes for MG RV8 colours are stamped on the VIN (Vehicle Identification Plates) - see table of chassis numbers

MGB GT V8: STANDARD UK PRODUCTION CHASSIS NUMBERS

G	D	2	D	1	*	G
MG	Engine over 3 litres	2 Door	GT Coupe	Right Hand Drive	Chassis sequence number: 101 - 1956 (chrome bumper); 2101 - 2632 or 2701 -2903	MG

MGB GT V8: US EXPORT SPECIFICATION CHASSIS NUMBERS

G	D	2	D	2	D	U	D	*	G
MG	engine over 3 litres	2 Door	GT Coupe	Left Hand Drive	Purpose unknown	USA	1973 Model year	Chassis sequence number: very few built (see separate table)	MG

MG RV8 VEHICLE IDENTIFICATION NUMBER (VIN)
(located at offside of bonnet slam panel)

S	A	R	RA	W	B	M	B	M	G	*
Geographic Area (South)	Country (UK)	Manufacturer (Rover)	Marque Model	Class	Body	Engine	Transmission and Steering	Model change	Assembly Plant (Cowley)	Serial Number (starting at 900000 for pre-production cars and 0000251 for customer cars)

MG RV8 PAINT & TRIM CODES AND LOCATION OF OTHER SERVICE NUMBERS

VIN PLATE PAINT & TRIM CODES						ENGINE NUMBER	GEARBOX NUMBER	REAR AXLE NUMBER	BODY NUMBER
TYPICAL PAINT CODES (at base of VIN Plate - see separate colour table for details of codes)			TRIM CODES (at base of VIN Plate; there is only one trim for the RV8, so only one code)			stamped on the cylinder block between numbers 3 and 5 cylinders (48A prefix means 3,948 cc, 9.35:1 CR, unleaded fuel and catalyst)	Stamped on the bottom RHS of the gearbox housing	Stamped on the rear face of the differential housing	Stamped on a plate fixed to the bonnet lock platform
BASIC COLOUR	MARQUE IDENTIFIER	COLOUR SHADE NAME	BASIC COLOUR	MARQUE IDENTIFIER	COLOUR SHADE NAME				
C	O	F	S	M	J				

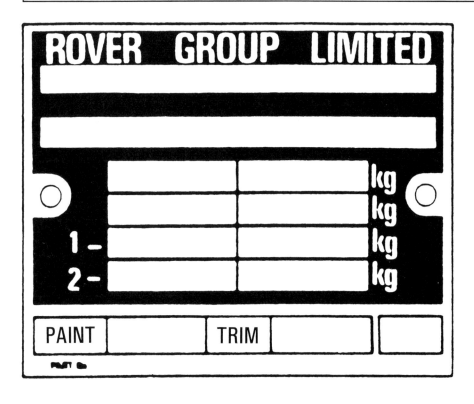

PERFORMANCE FIGURES - COSTELLO, MGB GT V8 & MG RV8					
	MGB GT V8 Costello	MGB GT V8 Costello	MGB GT V8	MGB GT V8	MG RV8
Magazine	Autocar	Motor	Motor	Autocar	Autocar & Motor
Date Published	25/5/1972	2/6/1973	25/8/1973	16/8/1973	16/6/1993
Maximum Speed (m.p.h.)	128	124	125	124	136
Acceleration through the gears in seconds: 0-30 m.p.h.	2.8	2.7	2.9	2.8	2.4
0-40	4.4	4.1	4.3	4.3	3.7
0-50	5.9	5.9	5.9	6.4	5.0
0-60	7.8	8.0	7.7	8.6	6.9
0-70	10.8	10.6	10.5	11.8	8.8
0-80	13.6	13.3	13.0	15.1	11.2
0-90	17.3	18.1	17.3	19.0	14.5
0-100	22.0	23.9	23.4	25.3	18.5
0-110	29.9	-	32.5	35.6	23.6
Acceleration in fourth in seconds: 10-30 m.p.h.	-	6.6	-	7.5	6.1
20-40	6.7	6.0	6.4	6.8	5.6
30-50	5.8	5.6	6.2	6.5	5.5
40-60	5.9	5.2	6.2	6.6	5.4
50-70	6.4	5.4	6.3	6.8	5.2
60-80	6.9	6.4	6.6	7.4	5.4
70-90	7.4	7.4	7.6	8.3	6.0
80-100	9.7	-	9.8	10.3	7.0
90-110	14.0	-	-	14.8	8.4
Overall fuel consumption (m.p.g.):	18.8 (5-Star 100 RON)	22.6 (5-Star 100 RON)	19.8 (3-Star 94 RON)	23.4 (3-Star 94 RON)	20.3 (Unleaded 95 RON)
Unladen weight (kg):	1041	not given	1077	1081	1101
Weight as tested (kg):	1215	not given	1265	1240	1101
Claimed Maximum Power:	150 b.h.p. (DIN) at 5,000 r.p.m.	150 b.h.p. (DIN) at 2,750 r.p.m.	137 b.h.p. (DIN) at 5,000 r.p.m.	137 b.h.p. (DIN) at 5,000 r.p.m.	190 b.h.p. at 4,750 r.p.m.
Claimed Maximum Torque:	201 lb.ft. at 2,750 r.p.m.	201 lb.ft. at 2,750 r.p.m.	193 lb.ft. at 2,900 r.p.m.	193 lb.ft. at 2,900 r.p.m.	234 lb.ft. at 3,200 r.p.m.

THE MGB GT V8 AND ITS RIVALS IN AUGUST 1973				
CAR	TOP SPEED * (mph)	0-60mph* (seconds)	ENGINE	PRICE £
MGB GT V8	124	8.2	3.5 V8	2294
MGB GT	106	12.0	1.8 S4	1575
FORD CAPRI 3000 GT	120	8.5	3.0 V6	1651
FORD CAPRI 3000 GXL	120	8.5	3.0 V6	1824
TVR 3000M	127	7.2	3.0 V6	2464
MORGAN PLUS 8	132	6.5	3.5 V8	1966
RELIANT SCIMITAR GTE	123	8.6	3.0 V6	2480
DATSUN 240Z	125	8.0	2.4 S6	2690
TRIUMPH STAG	120	9.0	3.0 V8	2615
LOTUS ELAN +2S 130	120	8.0	1.6 S4	2789
ALFA ROMEO GIULIA JUNIOR GT	115	11.0	1.6 S4	2349
ALFA ROMEO 2000 GTV	121	9.2	2.0 S4	2849
TRIDENT VENTURER	130	9.1	3.0 V6	2977
* Manufacturer's figures				

THE PRE-PRODUCTION MGB GT V8

Chassis Number	Body Colour/Trim	Steering	Original UK Reg. No.	Present Location	Current Reg. No.	Owner
GD2D2-100G	Flame/Navy	LHD	GON 943N	Switzerland	LU-104 228	Eric Prasse
GD2D1-99G	Blaze/Navy *	RHD	JBL 908L	United Kingdom	JBL 308L	Robin Dodson
GD2D2-98G	Teal Blue/Ochre	LHD	Not Registered	United States	Unknown	Lyle York
GD2D2-97G	Harvest Gold/Black	RHD	HUD 577N	United Kingdom	HUD 577N	Brian Field
GD2D1-96G	Glacier White/Navy	RHD	MMO 229L	United Kingdom	MMO 229L	Norman Ward
GD2D1-95G	Bronze Yellow/Navy	RHD	OBL 123L	Unknown	Unknown	Unknown

THE LEFT-HAND-DRIVE PRODUCTION MGB GT V8

Chassis Number	Body Colour/Trim	Steering	Original UK Reg. No.	Present Location	Current Reg. No.	Owner
GD2D2-DUD-101G	Green Mallard/Ochre	LHD	POR 222M	Switzerland	ZH-15027	Hans Hurzeler
GD2D2-DUD-102G	Glacier White/Navy	LHD	HUD 578N	Holland		Bas Geritts
GD2D2-DUD-104G	Blaze/Navy **	LHD	HUD 576N	Germany	OG-S-V80	Gerhard Maier
GD2D2-DUD-105G	Bronze Yellow/Navy	LHD	POL 862N	Holland	11-MS-70	J. W. Hamming
GD2D2-DUD-108G	Glacier White/Navy	LHD	HUD 575N	Holland	01-TH-83	Henk Boerboom
GD2D2-DUD-109G	Damask Red/Navy	LHD	POP 124M	Switzerland	ZH-376237	Thomas Studer
GD2D2-DUD-110G	Teal Blue/Ochre	LHD	NOP 554M	Switzerland	SG-66771	Roger Righini

*   The seats fitted to "Blaze ADO 75/413" were originally installed in this car, often referred to as "Flame 99" but, according to official records, finished in Blaze!
** Subsequently resprayed Glacier White by the current owner

THE MGB GT V8 DEVELOPMENT CARS

Chassis Number	Body Colour/Trim	Steering	Original UK Reg. No.	Present Location	Current Reg. No.	Owner
ADO 75/413	Blaze/Black *	RHD	URX 741N	United Kingdom	URX 741N	Graham Smith
ADO 75/414	Harvest Gold/Navy	RHD	Unknown	Unknown	Unknown	Unknown
ADO 75/424	Harvest Gold/Navy **	RHD	KBW 271S	United Kingdom	KBW 271S	Gordon Shepherd
ADO 75/425	Damask	Unknown	Unknown	Unknown	Unknown	Unknown
ADO 75/432 ***	Flamenco	RHD	WWL 79R	United Kingdom	WWL 79R	British Motor Heritage
ADO 75/433 ****	White	RHD	Unknown	Unknown	Unknown	Syd Beer

*   The seats fitted to "Blaze ADO 75/413" were originally installed in "Flame 99". This car had an interesting history, and fortunately for posterity the factory log book for it survived; it was fitted with the very first Rover "SD1" type V8 engines and used for early testing. The SD1 unit, however, was not destined for the MGB GT V8 production cars.
**   Now resprayed Austin-Morris "Denim Blue" Metallic
*** This car is described in the factory records, against the date of 8/10/75, as "RHD V8 Flamenco 1976 Hybrid" which means that it is almost certainly the car which subsequently bore the Chassis Number GD2D1-2903G, and which was the last production V8. The car forms part of the Heritage collection and is occasionally on show at their museum at Gaydon.
**** The factory record for this car, dated 10/10/75, describes it as "RHD V8 home [market]; re-designated O-series - facelift. This means that it is almost certainly the second-to last production chassis number, GD2D1-2902G.

THE MGB GT V8 PRESS CARS

Chassis Number	Body Colour/Trim	Steering	Original UK Reg. No.	Present Location	Current Reg. No.	Owner	Tested By ....
GD2D1-103G	Damask Red/Navy	RHD	* see footnotes			Michael Holmes	Original Damask photographic car
GD2D1-112G	Glacier White/Navy	RHD	GOF 88L	United Kingdom	GOF 88L	James Kelly	Police Review (car loaned to police)
GD2D1-113G	Bronze Yellow/Navy	RHD	HOH 903L	Holland		Willem D'Mol	Wheels 10/73, Road & Track 6/74
GD2D1-115G	Blaze/Navy	RHD	HOH 904L	United Kingdom	HOH 904L	Philip Armitage	
GD2D1-117G	Glacier White/Navy	RHD	HOH 905L		HOH 905L		
GD2D1-118G	Limeflower/Navy	RHD	HOH 901L	United Kingdom	HOH 901L	Mike Dunlop	CAR 9/73, Cars & Car Conversions
GD2D1-119G	Teal Blue/Ochre ** see footnotes	RHD	HOH 902L				What Car 11/73 *
GD2D1-120G	Black Tulip/Ochre	RHD	HOH 932L	United Kingdom	HOH 932L		Autosport 21/12/73 & Motorsport 10/73
GD2D1-121G	Blaze/Navy	RHD	HOH 919L				Motorsport 10/73, Autosport 21/12/73
GD2D1-124G	Green Mallard/Ochre	RHD	HOH 920L	United Kingdom	HOH 920L	Steve Cox	Autocar 16/8/73
GD2D1-130G	Harvest Gold/Navy	RHD	HOH 933L	United Kingdom	HOH 933L	Syd Beer	Motor 18 & 25/8/73 and 18/12/82, Classic Car 10/73
GD2D1-146G	Damask Red/Navy	RHD	HOH 934L	United Kingdom	HOH 934L	John Pfloumer	
GD2D1-2101G	Teal Blue/Autumn Leaf	RHD	TOF 560N	United Kingdom	TOF 560N	Jean Allen	Misc. photos, including 1976 Leyland Calendar and Autocar Sports Car Group Test of 5/4/75; first production R/B car
GD2D1-2102G	Harvest Gold/Black	RHD					Press Demonstrator
GD2D1-2103G	Mirage/Black	RHD					Used by B.L. Advertising

* Registration number unknown; this car was fitted with false plates for studio shots (see colour pages) and was the vehicle used for much of the original publicity shots, including brochure photographs.

** Although this car was Teal Blue, the car which appeared in colour on the front cover of "What Car" and bearing the registration number HOH 902L was Bronze Yellow, so the car tested by the magazine may in fact have been an incorrectly registered GD2D1-113G

A number of cars also appeared in the press with numbers which are not recorded. These registration numbers are of doubtful authenticity; "QPL 95N" is certainly false, as no UK registration numbers of that era ever commenced with a letter Q. Many cars were deliberately fitted with false numbers - obtained from the vehicle licensing authorities. Other numbers which appear but are of doubtful heritage include: YWL 667L; UOK 935L; AOG 740L; YWL 921L; NOJ 924M; AOL 750M; HUD 411M; EBO 173N; and UWL 747P.

THE MGB GT V8 MOTORSHOW CARS

Chassis Number	Body Colour/Trim	Steering	Original UK Reg. No.	Notes
1973 MOTOR SHOWS				
GD2D1-798G	Citron/Black	RHD	TOH 654N	Mounted on the assembly line on 21/9/73, this was Earls Court Show Car No. 23. "Show finish" less headlining. Invoiced when Austin Morris, Longbridge when built, later invoiced to Evans of Birmingham on 15/3/74. This was the car which was displayed on an angled frame over a sectioned V8 engine (see colour section).
GD2D1-799G	Aconite/Autumn Leaf	RHD	SGD 575N	Mounted on the assembly line on 3/10/73, this was Earls Court Show Car No. 27. Show finish and invoiced to Austin Morris Longbridge when built; later invoiced to Appleyard of Glasgow on 7/12/73
GD2D1-800G	Police White/Autumn Leaf	RHD	NOX 8M	Mounted on the assembly line on 1/10/73, this was Earls Court Show Car No. 43.
1974 MOTOR SHOWS				
GD2D1-841G	Aconite/Autumn Leaf	RHD		Mounted on the assembly line 18/10/73. This was 1974 Scottish Motor Show Car No. 6. Invoiced to Austin Morris Longbridge when built; later invoiced to Appleyard of Edinburgh.
GD2D1-2105G	Citron/Black	RHD		Mounted on the assembly line 20/9/74, this was Earls Court Motor Show Car No. 76. Invoiced to Austin Morris Longbridge when built; later invoiced to Newbury Motors, Aston, Birmingham.
GD2D1-2106G	Bracken/Autumn Leaf	RHD		Mounted on the assembly line on 20/9/74, this was Earls Court Show Car No. 97. Invoiced to Austin Morris Longbridge when built; later invoiced to Wadham Stringer of Guildford.
1975 MOTOR SHOWS				
GD2D1-2701G	Tahiti Blue/Autumn Leaf	RHD		Mounted on the assembly line on 12/9/75, this was Earls Court Show Car No. 28. Invoiced to Austin Morris Longbridge when built; later invoiced to Carlaw Cars of Glasgow.

THE MGB GT V8 POLICE CARS by Geoff Allen

Chassis Number	Body Colour/Trim	Original UK Reg. No.	NOTES
THE MGB GT V8 DEMONSTRATION POLICE CARS			
GD2D1-112G	Police White/Navy	GOF 88L	Mounted on the assembly line on 30/1/73, this car did not finally pass through paint finishing and invoicing for sale until 1/11/73, which was probably the point when the car was disposed of as a second-hand sale. This car was originally invoiced to Austin Morris UK home sales, Longbridge and through Fleet Sales it was on loan to the police for a period, during which time it featured in a report by "Police Review" magazine. "Police White" was used for many years on various models supplied to the Bradford Police and the colour was more correctly known as "Bradford Police White" even though it was used by other forces.
GD2D1-800G	Police White/ Autumn Leaf	NOX 8M	Mounted on the assembly line on 1/10/73, this car was one of the three Earls Court Show Models for 1973 and was displayed by Hoffman Balancing Techniques. It received an award in the bodywork section for cars in its price range. Later, through Austin Morris Publicity, it was transferred to the police, probably at the date of invoicing after the show (9/1/73). At one time it had, fitted on the centre of the roof, a triangular roof illuminated "Police" sign with a rotating blue light but this appears to have been quickly removed; in fact it may only have been tried in the factory. In show guise it had two 18" strip lights fitted inside - one each side on the cant-rails over the doors - as was more or less standard on MGB GT show models at that time. The car is at present (1993) painted blue and has a sunroof fitted.
THE OPERATIONAL MGB GT V8 POLICE CARS			
GD2D1-1006G	Blaze/Black	TBH 355M	Mounted on the assembly line on 14/11/73 and invoiced to the Stevenage Motor Co. Ltd. on 19/11/73. The present owner gives the date of first registration as 17/6/74.
GD2D1-1036G	Citron/Black	PPP 99M	Mounted on the assembly line on 28/11/73 and invoiced to Lex Garages of Gloucester on 4/12/73. First registration date is unknown; the current registration is PRJ 426M.
GD2D1-1378G	Bracken/ Autumn Leaf	VBH 920M	Mounted on the assembly line on 14/2/74 and invoiced to Kennings of Norwich on 18/3/73.

The three "Operational Police Cars" listed (known as "Q" Cars at the time) were used by the Thames Valley Police during 1974 and possibly 1975. They were fitted with standard Police two-tone horns and carried no external markings. On the rear compartment platform a retractable "STOP - POLICE" sign was fitted, operated by the crew pulling a cord which rotated the sign out of its box and at the same time illuminating it. Fairly early in the life of the cars one lost several teeth from third gear, in turn splitting the gearbox casing. After fitting a new gearbox all three cars had the overdrive wiring disconnected. One local show-biz personality wrote to "Motorsport" at the time, complaining that he had been chased by an MGB GT V8 which overtook him and raised the "STOP - POLICE" sign; he warned other road users to beware of this car. The factory grapevine at the time of the demise of the V8 suggested that the police had asked BL to build three more V8's to replace theirs; however, it was too late as the build was about to finish. All three cars were eventually sold off after covering over 80,000 miles, sold by auction for £2,150.96, £2,159.96 and £2,243.53 respectively. The two factory produced cars probably had the "Smiths Police calibrated speedometers" fitted in the Abingdon factory. In the case of the other three cars used by Thames Valley Police, these speedometers were probably fitted at the Police Vehicle Workshops at Kidlington.

© GEOFF ALLEN

MGB & MGB GT V8 DEVELOPMENT "EX REGISTER" PROJECT CODES		
Code	Date	Subject [author's notes in square brackets]
EX205		**MG TWO SEATER (ADO23) - Transferred into ADO23 Book**
EX205/1	-	1/4" scale body arrangement [Jim O'Neill's coupe design]
EX205/2	20/6/57	Scale body arrangement - Frua body on MGA chassis [The Frua bodied MGA]
EX205/3	20/6/57	Scale body arrangement (based on the previous two)
EX205/4	3/1/58	Brake Pedal
EX205/5	3/1/58	Clutch Pedal RH
EX205/6	3/1/58	Clutch Pedal LH
EX205/7	3/2/58	Arrangement - jacking bracket
EX205/8	3/2/58	Inner jacking bracket - RH
EX205/9	3/2/58	Inner jacking bracket - LH
EX205/10	3/2/58	Outer jacking bracket
EX205/11	3/2/58	Tube jacking bracket
EX214		**REPLACEMENT FOR MGA - BODY FACELIFT, WINGS ETC.**
EX214/1	9/6/58	1/4 Scale body lines
EX214/2	13/6/58	Scheme for V4 engine installation in 91" wheelbase
EX214/3	17/6/58	Scheme for Twin Cam engine installation in 91" wheelbase
EX214/4	20/6/58	Scheme for 2-Litre engine (as 2.9 litre engine with Nos. 3 & 4 cylinders missing), installed in 91" wheelbase
EX214/5	-	Scheme for MG 2-litre engine installed in 91" wheelbase
EX214/6	20/10/58	Scheme 1 for MGB V4
EX214/7	20/10/58	Scheme 2 for MGB V4
EX214/8	7/11/58	Scheme 3 for MGB V4
EX214/9	5/1/59	Sill section (showing welding conditions) [note added stating "s/s AD023"]
EX214/10	3/2/59	1/4" scale body lines - twin headlamps and revised rear wing [drawing shows coupe similar to EX205/1 with narrowed MGB type grille and twin headlamps in widened MGB type nacelles]
EX214/11	19/2/59	1/4" scale body lines - wide radiator grille - short coupe top (rear end as EX214/1)
EX214/12	1/5/59	1/4" scale body lines - wide radiator grille [drawing itself renumbered as ADO23/168]
EX249		**"ADO 23 ROVER V8"**
EX249/1	5/8/71	Clutch Scheme [first drawing listed]
EX249/104	14/1/72	[last entry under EX249; total of 439 drawings including those for ADO75 by the time that the MGB GT V8 was launched]

MGB GT V8 PRODUCTION CHANGES

The table below list the various official chassis number change points; more comprehesive coverage is given in Volume 5 of the V8 Register's "Workshop Notes". The MGB GT V8 production cars started with suffix "-101" and ended with suffix "-2903", the prefixes in all RHD cases being "GD2D1-". Note that some change points were not recorded and others may not have been rigidly applied in practice (see notes at end of table)

CHASSIS NUMBER GD2D1-****G	NATURE OF CHANGES
101	FIRST PRODUCTION CAR PRODUCED IN DECEMBER 1972. CAR LAUNCHED TO PUBLIC IN AUGUST 1973
???	DOOR WAIST RAIL CAPPING CHANGED
349	DOOR WAIST RAIL CAPPING CHANGED
490	HEATED REAR WINDOW SWITCH CHANGED ("HEATED BACKLIGHT SWITCH")
608	DOOR MIRRORS CHANGED FOR FIRST TIME (SEE 2823)
650	WINDSCREEN WASHER ELECTRIC PUMP CHANGED
754	REAR SEAT SQUAB HINGE CHANGED
799	CARPET BUTTON (FOR BOOT SIDE COMPARTMENTS) CHANGED
1149	CHANGE TO OIL TEMPERATURE GAUGE TAKE OFF - MOVED FROM REMOTE OIL FILTER TO OIL PUMP
1248	REAR NUMBER PLATE LIGHTS MOVED FROM OVERRIDERS TO BUMPER
1424	JACK CHANGED AND COMMONISED WITH A NEW JACK FOR 1800 CARS
1720	FRONT & REAR BRAKE HOSES CHANGED
1825	OIL PRESSURE / WATER TEMPERATURE GAUGE CHANGED
1955	SUN VISORS CHANGED
1956	LAST CHROME BUMPER V8; NO CARS BUILT WITH NUMBERS 1957 TO 2100 INCLUSIVE
2101	FIRST "RUBBER BUMPER" V8; CAR EXTENSIVELY REVISED ALONG WITH MGB 1800 RANGE TO COMPLY WITH US IMPACT LEGISLATION
2146	HEATER WATER VALVE CHANGED
2186	WINDSCREEN WIPER WHEEL BOX CHANGED
2199	HEAD RESTRAINT FRICTION ROLLERS & STEERING WHEEL BOSS ALTERED
2205	MODIFICATION TO FRONT SUSPENSION - DISTANCE TUBE LINK CHANGED
2292	HEATER CONTROL CABLE CHANGED
2530	FRONT AND REAR BUMPER ARMATURES MODIFIED
2618	FURTHER MINOR CHANGES TO FRONT BUMPER
2632	LAST CAR OF 1975 MODEL YEAR; NO CARS BUILT WITH NUMBERS 2633 - 2700 INCLUSIVE
2701	NEW (1976) MODEL YEAR: BODYSHELL CHANGED, PETROL TANK FILLER ORIFICE MODIFIED, INNER WING MODIFIED, BONNET STAY SPACER CHANGED & HANDBRAKE MECHANISM ALTERED
2708	FRONT BRAKE HOSE CHANGED FOR SECOND TIME
2713	FURTHER MODIFICATION TO PETROL FILLER ARRANGEMENTS - FILLER NECK MODIFIED
2723	MINOR TRIM AND BADGE REVISIONS
2742	STARTER RELAY CHANGED
2823	DOOR MIRRORS CHANGED FOR SECOND TIME (SEE 608)
2903	LAST CAR PRODUCED IN SEPTEMBER 1976

MGB GT V8 PRODUCTION CHANGES

FURTHER NOTES ON CHANGES DURING THE PRODUCTION LIFE OF THE MGB GT V8

1. **OTHER CHANGES WHICH TOOK PLACE BUT FOR WHICH NO RELIABLE INFORMATION ON CHANGE POINTS EXIST**

1.1 **Gearbox Selector** The very early production cars were fitted with the contemporary MGB (1800) gearbox selector which meant that overdrive was available on both third and fourth gears. The MGB item was 22B386 and this was replaced by 22B726 on most production cars. Additionally, the gearbox "Plunger isolation switch" was changed from 22B406 to 22B727, the nett effect being that most V8's only have overdrive on top gear.

1.2 **Air Cleaner Fixings** On early cars (including those used for publicity photographs and by the technical illustrators who prepared workshop manuals and handbooks for the V8), an additional clip GHC1622 was fitted to secure each of the "lobster claw" air cleaner units to the back air cleaner box. In the majority of cases, production cars only had these clips fitted to secure the temperature sensitive air valves to the ends of the "lobster claws"; i.e. only two number GHC1622 rather than four number.

1.3 **Brake Master Cylinder** This was changed from GMC122 to GMC150, and the different types may be identified by concentric rings on the latter.

1.4 **Bonnet Panel** This was commonised with the MGB panel, since the V8 bonnet required a greater curvature than the contemporary MGB bonnet at the time of the V8 launch. This was to allow clearance over the carburettors. Thus the old MGB bonnet (HZA4015) and the original V8 bonnet (HZA4197) were both replaced by HZA4014.

1.5 **Badge and trim changes** The first "rubber bumper" V8's had silver metal "MG" badges set in the centre of the front bumper unit. These had a scarlet background. The same "BGT" tailgate badge as the chrome bumper cars (i.e. with a blue "GT" flash) was fitted and the V8 badges reduced from three to two (one the nearside wing and the left hand side of the tailgate). This continued throughout 1974. However, 1975 was decreed by BL as "MG Golden Jubilee Year" and it was decided to celebrate this by changing the finish of the nose, tail and "V" badges from silver to a pale gold. (Nose badge CHA507, tailgate "BGT" badge HZA5023, V8 L.H. Wing Badge HZA5021 and V8 Tailgate Badge HZA5022). The red background of the nose badge was changed to black, and the blue flash of the "BGT" tailgate badge was changed to black. For the 1976 model year, the finish reverted to silver but the black background was retained for the new version of the nose badge (CHA544) and also the flash on the tailgate "BGT" badge. No reliable chassis number change points have been recorded to determine exactly when these changes took place, and therefore the "official" change point details given in the table (for Chassis Number 2723) should not be regarded as accurate.

1.6 **Police Speedometer** Police specification V8s were fitted with a specially calibrated speedometer (BHA5317) instead of BHA5210

1.7 **Front and rear valances** When the black bumpers were first introduced in October 1974, the front and rear valances, beneath the bumper units, continued to be finished in the appropriate body colour. However at some point the valances were mask-sprayed in satin black, presumably in an attempt to harmonise the appearance of the heavy bumper units. The paint used had no special properties such as impact resistance, and was very thinly applied, so the probability is that it purpose was purely cosmetic. The point at which this change took place is a little uncertain - it seems to have been applied from around the beginning of the 1976 Model Year, when the "C-Pillar" trims were first fitted (Chassis No. 2723) but as so many cars have been restored and their valances replaced it is difficult to be certain.

2. **CHANGES ON FINAL TWO CARS BUILT (CHASSIS NUMBERS GD2D1-2902 & 2903)** The final two cars, "White 2902" and "Flamenco 2903", were built with the final facelift bodyshell launched for the MGB 1800 range in July 1976. The changes were to the interior (where the new dashboard with plastic panel and illuminated rocker switches was fitted, but using the conventional V8 speedometer and tachometer. The interior trim was carried over from the earlier specification, rather than the new "deckchair" fabric adopted for the face-lifted 1977 model year 1800 range. The later bodyshell also incorporated brackets for the rear anti-roll bar but this was not fitted. These cars were modified in this way in the hope that BL would give the V8 a "stay of execution" - but unfortunately to no avail!

3. **GENERAL NOTES ON THE RELIABILITY OF THE CHASSIS NUMBER CHANGE POINTS GIVEN IN THE TABLE ABOVE (By Geoff Allen)** Most of the Chassis Number change points are fairly flexible as parts were changed by both the Assembly Line Rectifiers and the Major Rectification Department. The car numbers were not circulated with particular regularity and there was also a tendency for odd boxes of parts to turn up from time to time. For example, at one stage a box containing around fifty rear bumpers was discovered underneath a bench and consequently the Chassis Change point (GD2D1-1248) is not reliable since there was a considerable overlap!

MG RV8 PRE-PRODUCTION DEVELOPMENT AND VALIDATION CARS

VEHICLE I.D.	BUILD REFERENCE	VIN NUMBER (if known)	REGISTRATION NUMBER	COLOUR	NOTES
DEVELOPMENT CARS					
ZZ 2841	ADD DEV01	n/a	LFC 436S	BMH GREEN	The original BMH development car, built by Mark Gamble using a white MGB roadster body, and known as "DEV-1". Uprated to 3.5 litre Land Rover V8 engine and subsequently upgraded to 3.9 litre V8 and suspension and brakes modified. Later became styling vehicle, with clay shaped over basic bodyshell.
ZZ 2842	ADD DEV02	n/a	YWU 486S	RED	MGB basis as for "DEV-1" and known as "DEV-2". Uprated in similar manner to DEV-1 and used for engine cooling test. Car resides at Gaydon as of late 1993.
ZZ 2843	ADD DEV03	n/a	JGT 808N	WHITE	This is the car "scooped" by CAR magazine in their June 1992 issue.
ZZ 2844	ADD DEV04	n/a	Unregistered	WHITE	Vehicle used for rig test
VALIDATION CARS					
ADD 1	ADD VAL01		SFH 639W	RED	Rear axle test; misuse and abuse, stop-start transmission testing. MGB body.
ADD 2	ADD VAL02		TAD 92W	BLACK	60,000 mile durability test. Car assessed by "CAR magazine in November 1992 issue (see colour photo section). MGB body, RV8 wheels.
ADD 3	ADD VAL03	900000	K638 WOK	FLAME RED	First RV8 "Adder" built. Specification test-car.
ADD 4	ADD VAL04	900001	K637 WOK	NIGHTFIRE	High speed test-car and electrical test.
ADD 5	ADD VAL05	900002	K377 CAC	BRITISH RACING GREEN	Chassis test car; Longbridge.
ZZ 2951	ADD VAL06		Unregistered	Unpainted	"Body-in-white" (bare shell) for body kit development.
ZZ 2952	ADD VAL07	900008	K140 CDU	LE MANS GREEN	Photographic car used for MG RV8 brochure (see colour photo section) and subsequently used in hillclimb competition by Dave Peers of RSP. This was the first complete RV8 built - i.e. the first car to feature correct body, engine, interior trim etc. to production specification.
ZZ 2954	ADD VAL09 *		Unregistered	WHITE	Manufacturing - trim development.
ZZ 2957	ADD VAL12		Unregistered	WHITE GOLD	Crash test vehicle
ZZ 2958	ADD VAL13	900006	K251 CDU	LE MANS GREEN	Customer viewing, dealer support, TV car for drama series "Peak Practice".
ZZ 2959	ADD VAL14		Unregistered	LE MANS GREEN	1992 Motor Show Car (Birmingham NEC, Geneva, MG Day)
ADD 101	ADD 101	900009	K139 CDU	CARIBBEAN BLUE	Specification testing; figure of eight and pave.
ADD 201	ADD 201		Unregistered	CARIBBEAN BLUE	Homologation cars and service training.
ADD 202	ADD 202	900010	K317 EHP	NIGHTFIRE	Brake testing. It is believed that this car has been broken up.
ADD 204	ADD 204		Unregistered	DIAMOND WHITE	Pave testing.
ZZ 3883	ADD 205		Unregistered	DIAMOND WHITE	Hood development.
ZZ 3428	ADD 301	900012	K398 FDU	WOODCOTE GREEN	Durability car and team use.
ADD302	ADD 302		Unregistered	LE MANS GREEN	Belfast Motor Show and dealer demonstration car.
ADD303	ADD 303		Reg. in Japan	BRITISH RACING GREEN	Japanese specification car; air conditioning testing.
ZZ 3884	ADD 304		Unregistered	DIAMOND WHITE	Slam test.
ZZ 4507	ADD 401	900003	K574 FKV	BLACK	18,000 mile durability testing, then team demonstration.
ZZ 4642	ADD 402	900025	K17 MGR	OXFORD BLUE	Dealer demonstration car
ZZ 4630	ADD 403	900016	K6 MGR	OLD ENGLISH WHITE	Dealer demonstration car
ZZ 4633	ADD 404		Unregistered	BRITISH RACING GREEN	Australian specification car
ZZ 4644	ADD 405	900022	K70 MGR	OXFORD BLUE	Dealer demonstration car
ZZ 4645	ADD 406	900015	K60 MGR	BRITISH RACING GREEN	Dealer demonstration car
ZZ 4631	ADD 407	900020	K20 MGR	LE MANS GREEN	Dealer demonstration car
ZZ 4632	ADD 408	900018	K18 MGR	NIGHTFIRE	Dealer demonstration car
ZZ 4646	ADD 501	900028	K13 MGR	CARIBBEAN BLUE	Dealer demonstration car
ADD 502	ADD 502	900019	K16 MGR	LE MANS GREEN	Dealer demonstration car. This car was used for the Central TV comedy series "Law & Disorder", starring Penelope Keith as a barrister.
ADD 503	ADD 503	900021	K11 MGR	NIGHTFIRE	Dealer demonstration car
ADD 504	ADD 504	900023	K90 MGR	OXFORD BLUE	Dealer demonstration car
ZZ 4550	ADD 505	900026	K50 MGR	LE MANS GREEN	Dealer demonstration car
ZZ 4651	ADD 506	900027	K19 MGR	LE MANS GREEN	Dealer demonstration car
ZZ 4759	ADD 507	900030	K15 MGR	WHITE GOLD	Dealer demonstration car
ZZ 4653	ADD 508	900029	K12 MGR	NIGHTFIRE	Press Car - tested by "Autocar & Motor", "What Car?" etc.; see colour pages in this book
ZZ 4694	ADD 509	900017	K14 MGR	WOODCOTE GREEN	Press Car - featured on the cover of this book
Information supplied by Mark Gamble, RSP					* ADD VAL08, 10 & 11 Not built

MG RV8
FIRST PRODUCTION AND PRESS CARS

Registration Number	VIN Number	Colour	Notes
K60 MGR	900015	British Racing Green	
K6 MGR	900016	Old English White	
K14 MGR	900017	Woodcote Green	Press Car: see cover photo
K18 MGR	900018	Nightfire Red	
K16 MGR	900019	Le Mans Green	
K20 MGR	900020	Le Mans Green	
K11 MGR	900021	Nightfire Red	
K70 MGR	900022	Oxford Blue	
K17 MGR	900025	Oxford Blue	
K50 MGR	900026	Le Mans Green	
K19 MGR	900027	Le Mans Green	
K13 MGR	900028	Oxford Blue	
K12 MGR	900029	Nightfire Red	Tested by many magazines; see colour pages
K15 MGR	900030	White Gold	
K536 JRW	000251	British Racing Green	The first customer car, now in the BMH collection at Gaydon

Notes: 1). There have only been two official RV8 Press Cars - K12 MGR & K14 MGR, although other cars have occasionally appeared in the press.

2). A Le Mans Green car bearing the false photographic registration plate "K417 DCY" appeared on the front cover of "CAR" magazine in the November 1992 issue. This car was in fact K140 CDU, the car used for brochure photography and now raced by Dave Peers of RSP, but at that stage it had not been registered, hence the false number plates.

Right: John Towers, Rover Group Managing Director, hands the keys of the first production MG RV8 to Peter Mitchell, Managing Director of the British Motor Industry Heritage Trust.

MGB GT V8 & MG RV8 SALES LITERATURE CHECKLIST

Publication Number	Date of Issue	Cover Text, slogan	Notes
MGB GT V8			
2962/A	July 1973	MGB GT & V8 "MG The Great British Sports Car"	MGB GT & V8 only
2962/B	Early 1974	As above, basically a simple reprint with few changes	
3023	July 1973	"The New MGB GT V8"	50,000 print order
3037	Summer 1973	"The Great British Sports Car · MG"	Full MG range
3037/A	Early 1974	As above; few changes	
3054	September 1974	"You Can Do It in an MG"	Full MG range; 160,000 print order
3054/A	February 1975	As above; few changes	50,000 print order
3089	October 1974	MGB GT & V8	First "black bumper" 150,000 print order
3089/A	May 1975	As above; few changes	150,000 print order
3089/B	March 1976	As above; rare final reprint	25,000 print order
3148	Autumn 1975	"MG The Freeway"	Full MG range (print order unknown)
3148/A	Late 1975	As above; minor changes	
3148/B	March 1976	As above; minor changes	Final V8 appearance in range brochure; 35,000 print order
MG RV8			
4343	June 1992	"MG RV8 · The Shape of Things to Come	3 page double-sided folder
No number	June 1992	As above	As above but with tear-off slip
4401	October 1992	"MG RV8 · Colours and Trims"	2 page colour and trim card
4405	October 1992	"MG RV8 · The Marque Has Returned"	30 page large format brochure
4406	October 1992	"MG 1930-1992 · The History of The Marque"	Historical review of MG marque
4429	October 1992	"MG Classic Collection"	Includes 4427, 4428 or 4428/A price list
4441	End of 1992	"MG RV8 · The Marque Has Returned"	18 page smaller format brochure

MGB GT V8 & MG RV8 SERVICE LITERATURE CHECKLIST

Publication Number	Date of Issue	Subject	Notes
MGB GT V8			
AKD8423	1973	MGB GT V8 DRIVER'S HANDBOOK	Listed in the official Rover list as "MGB V8 RHD", showing that a LHD car was still regarded as a possibility. Revised several times and never superseded as the V8 handbook.
AKD8450	Not issued	REPAIR OPERATION MANUAL · MGB V8	This would have been the workshop manual specific to the MGB GT V8
AKD8461	Not issued	PROVISIONAL REPAIR OPERATION MANUAL · MGB V8	As for AKD8450
AKD8463	1973	REPAIR OPERATION TIMES · MGB V8 U.K.	These cards were commonly produced for all BL cars as a guide for the time which various basic service operations should take · and hence give a guide to service charges for the customer.
AKD8468	1973	WORKSHOP MANUAL SUPPLEMENT	When the MG V8 Workshop Manual did appear, it was as a supplement to the contemporary revision of the main MGB Workshop Manual (AKD3259) rather than as a manual in its own right.
AKD8470	1st MAY 1973	DATA CARD	This was a compact (105mm wide x 150mm high) card which listed the basic service data relevant to the car · e.g. oil capacity, tyre pressures and so forth. On the reverse was printed the equivalent MGB data.
AKM0039	1973	MGB & MGB GT V8 PARTS CATALOGUE	This invaluable document lists every service component, together with its appropriate Part Number. It is a very useful adjunct to the Workshop Manual and fortunately reprints are now available.
AKM3312	1974/5	MGB GT V8 PLUSPART LIST	The "PlusPart" accessories grew out of Leyland Special Tuning · which was of course based at the Abingdon M.G. factory. If anyone has one of these documents, it would be nice to see it!
AKM3461	1975/6	REPAIR OPERATION TIMES · SPRITE/ MIDGET/ MGB/ MGB V8	
MG RV8			
AKM7144	1993	OWNER'S HANDBOOK	This beautifully presented manual, supplied to the owner as part of a set of documents in a handsome leather wallet, follows the style of the contemporary sales literature for the RV8 · a plain white cover with the new style bronze and brown M.G. badge.
AKM7150	1993	SERVICE RECORD	Matching the Handbook in size and style, this is the service book in which the dealer stamps to certify that servicing has been carried out.
AKM7153	1993	REPAIR MANUAL	Roughly the same overall size as this book, this comprehensive loose-leaf document covers all servicing aspects of the RV8.
AKM7158	1993	OWNER'S INFORMATION PORTFOLIO	This is a further document which matches the handbook, and contains such information as service requirements, a list of Rover dealers and a useful UK map section, similar to that in AA handbooks.

SPECIALIST SERVICES AND SUPPLIERS

Name	Address	Category
Brown & Gammons Ltd.	18 High Street, Baldock, Hertfordshire SG7 6AS	Heritage Approved Major MG spares and restoration specialist.
MOSS Europe Ltd.	H/O at Victoria Villas, Richmond-upon-Thames, Surrey TW9 2JX; retail premises at nearby Manor Road, Richmond and also in: Bristol, Birmingham, Manchester, Shipley and Darlington	Heritage Approved Major MG spares specialist.
M&G International	International House, Lord Street, Birkenhead, Merseyside L41 1HT	Heritage Approved Major MG spares specialist.
Ron Hopkinson MG Parts Centre	850 London Road, Derby, DE2 8WA	Heritage Approved Major MG spares specialist.
Bromsgrove MG Centre	Unit 10, Sugarbrook Road, Aston Fields Industrial Estate, Bromsgrove, B61 3DW	MGB, MGC & MGB GT V8 spares specialist. Exclusive parts remanufactured.
John Hill's MGB Centre	Arthur Street, Redditch, Worcs. B98 8JY	Major MGB spares specialist.
Geoff Allen	61 Northcourt Road, Abingdon, Oxon OX14 1NR	Servicing and restoration by a former MG employee and leading MG V8 expert.
Mike Satur - Hands Down Ltd.	27 Crabtree Drive, Great Houghton, Barnsley, S72 0AF	Custom trimming for all MG's, including walnut dasboards for the MGB GT V8.
LV Engineering (Robbie Shaerf)	11 West Hampstead Mews, London NW6 3BB	Spares, servicing and expert restoration
Real Steel	Unit 9, Tomo Industrial Estate, Packet Boat Lane, Cowley, Uxbridge, Middx. UB8 2JP	Rover V8 engine parts specialists
Costello Engineering	3 Darns Hill, Crockenhill, Swanley, Kent BR8 8LQ	"Costello" MG V8 conversions & gearboxes
Peter Burgess	Unit 1, Amber Buildings, Meadow Lane, Alfreton, Derbyshire	V8 cylinder head improvements and engine restorations
Mike the Pipe (Mike Randall)	128 Stanley Park Road, Wallington, Surrey	V8 tubular exhaust fabricators
Brooklands Books	PO Box 146, Cobham, Surrey KT11 1LG	MG V8 workshop manuals, handbooks, parts manuals and road tests.
Beer of Houghton	Houghton, Huntingdon, Cambridgeshire PE17 2BD	MG V8 service, racing and restorations.
V8 Conversion Co. (Dave Vale)	123 High Street, Farnborough, Kent, BR6 7AZ	MGB V8 conversions and parts for conversions
MG Centre, St. Louis, USA (Robin Weatherall)	8370 Olive Boulevard, St. Louis, Missouri, MO 63130, USA	MGB V8 conversions - including US agent for Costello MGB V8
Clive Wheatley MG V8 Parts	The Garage, 2 Chequer Street, Penn Fields, Wolverhampton, West Midlands, WV3 7DL	Specialist in MG V8 parts - including remanufacture of the unique MG V8 rocker covers.
Vanderburg Spares (Hans and Coby Vanderburg)	Ploegveld 37, 5261 GD Vught, Holland	leading Dutch MG V8 sales, service and restoration experts
Moto-Build	328 Bath Road, Hounslow, Middlesex	Spares, servicing, sales and tuning
Oselli Engineering	Ferry Hinksey Road, Oxford, OX2 0BY	Leading performance engine experts
Sportscar Workshop	Turnham Green Terrace Mews, Chiswick, London W4	Restoration & servicing
The Huntsman Garage (Dave Franklin)	Westerleigh Road, Downend, Bristol	MGB V8 conversions and servicing

The V8 Register, The MG Car Club and Others

The V8 Register was founded in the autumn of 1978 by Victor Smith, the current Registrar. Along with other MGB GT V8 owners, Victor recognised the need for a specialised forum dedicated to the welfare and interests of V8-engined MGB owners, whether their cars were factory-built or privately converted. There was never any snobbish bias against conversions, which right from the outset the V8 Register has welcomed irrespective of parentage.

In the early days, the V8 Register produced its own colour newsletter, *The V8 Journal* — an ambitious undertaking for what was, after all, a relatively small register under the wing of the MG Car Club.

Of particular concern to Victor Smith was the availability of parts for the V8: many of them were unique and, because of the car's low production total, there was a serious possibility that owners might be forced to take their cars off the road or modify them with substitute parts. As a means of solving the problem before it occurred, a core group of MG specialists with a particular interest in the V8-engined MGB was recruited, including David Franklin and Beer of Houghton, to form the 'V8 Lifeline'. One of the earliest products offered by the V8 Register itself was the 'V8 Engine Life-saver Kit', comprising nothing more than a small nut which should be fitted to a redundant bolt on the V8 carburettor airbox to prevent it falling into the engine — which, as some owners had already discovered, could cause major trouble and expense!

Concern with the maintenance and improvement of the MGB V8 has been one of the consistent themes of the Register and is reflected in its motto, 'Maintaining The Breed', after John Thornley's much-reprinted MG history. Its 'Workshop Notes', which appear regularly in the MG Car Club magazine *Safety Fast*, have passed on countless hints and tips from Register members and have provided sufficient material for the publishing of no less than five compilations, three of which have sold out and are now keenly sought. In more recent years, a similar series of 'Concours Notes' has been appearing in the magazine, and will no doubt also be published in book form.

Aside from these technical considerations, the V8 Register has a busy social calendar, with gatherings which range from an informal 'Curry Evening' to major participation in the MGCC's annual Silverstone 'International'.

The Register offers a wide range of exclusive regalia to V8 enthusiasts, among which are clothing (including 'MG V8 Anniversary' T-shirts), footwell mats, key-fobs, enamel V8 lapel badges and tax-disc holders.

The MGCC V8 Register's parent organisation, the MG Car Club, was founded in 1930 and retained close ties with the MG Car Company until 1969 when British Leyland severed all official links with motoring clubs. Until the mid-1970s the MGCC tended to emphasise the competition side of MG activities, but since then has increasingly recognised the non-racing aspects of the marque. It now includes 13 Registers, catering for every MG from 14/40 to RV8.

The MG Owners' Club, founded in 1973, caters to MG Midget, MGB, MGC and V8 devotees and has grown over the years to become the largest single-marque club in the world. The MGOC offers a vast range of services, including insurance and a full-colour monthly magazine.

In North America, the number of regional MG clubs is almost infinite, but the principal one for V8 enthusiasts is the North American MGB Register — NAMGBR. Based in Akin, Illinois, the Register was founded in 1990 and takes in the entire North American continent. A professionally produced bi-monthly magazine is issued to members and is packed with both news and maintenance tips. There are registrars for each category of MGB, including the V8, and membership is rapidly growing.

As a general rule, highway regulations prohibit the use of signposts on which specific companies or organisations are referred to by name. There are exceptions, however, as is proved by this signposting of the Abingdon-based MG Car Club. (David Knowles)

ADDRESSES:

MG Car Club (including the V8 Register), Kimber House, PO Box 251, Abingdon, Oxfordshire OX14 1FF.

MG Owners' Club, Octagon House, Swavesey, Cambridgeshire CB4 5QZ.

North American MGB Register, PO Box MGB, Akin, IL 62805, USA.

BIBLIOGRAPHY

MGB Histories

Mighty MGs. *Graham Robson.* David & Charles.
The MGA, MGB & MGC: A Collector's Guide. *Graham Robson.*
Motor Racing Publications.
MG: The A, B And C. *Chris Harvey.* Haynes Publishing.
MGA, MGB & MGC. *Martin Buckley.* Hamlyn Publishing.
MGB: The Illustrated History. *Jonathan Wood & Lionel Burrell.* Haynes Publishing.
MGB: The Complete Story. *Brian Laban.* The Crowood Press.
MGB Super Profile. *Lindsay Porter.* Haynes Publishing.

MGB Buying, Restoration, Modification

MGB: Guide To Purchase & DIY Restoration. *Lindsay Porter.* Haynes Publishing.
MGB Uprating & Bodyshell Rebuild. *Practical Classics.* Kelsey Publishing.
MGB Restoration/Preparation/Maintenance. *Jim Tyler.* Osprey Publishing.
Improve & Modify MGB. *Lindsay Porter & Dave Pollard.* Haynes Publishing.
MGB, MGC & MGB GT V8 1962-1980: Choice, Purchase & Performance.
Chris Horton. Windrow & Greene.

General MG Histories

MG By McComb. *F. Wilson McComb.* Osprey Publishing.
MG: The Art Of Abingdon. *John McLellan.* Motor Racing Publications.
MG: The Magic of The Marque. *Mike Allison.* Dalton Watson.
Advertising MG, Volume II, 1956-1992. *Daniel Young.* Yesteryear Books.

Road Tests

MGB, MGC & V8 Gold Portfolio 1962-1980. Brooklands Books.
Road & Track On MG Sports Cars. Brooklands Books.

Factory Literature

MG MGB 1968-1981 Official Owner's Workshop Manual. Brooklands Books.
MGB GT V8 Official Workshop Manual Supplement. Brooklands Books.
MGB Tourer, GT & V8 Official Parts Catalogue. Brooklands Books.
MG MGB GT V8 Official Driver's Handbook. Brooklands Books.
MGB Heritage Portfolio. Sales brochures. Bay View Books.

The V8 Engine

The Rover V8 Engine. *David Hardcastle.* Haynes Publishing.
Tuning Rover V8 Engines. *David Hardcastle.* Haynes Publishing.

Note: The majority of these books are in print at time of writing.
Out-of-print titles can often be found at autojumbles or through
the secondhand motoring book specialists who advertise regularly
in leading classic car journals.

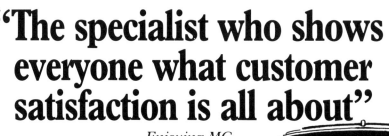

THE MG CAR CLUB
THE BEST CAR CLUB FOR YOU AND YOUR MG

Join the M.G. Car Club **NOW** and you will discover a whole new way to enjoy your MG.

The M.G. Car Club was established over 60 years ago. We are the friendly club and we have the experience and the know-how to help you to enjoy owning and running your M.G.

* Activities for all ages and tastes : social, touring, concours, autotests, sprints to full race

* Award winning, full colour monthly magazine - "Safety Fast" - packed full with features, technical tips, reports

* Technical aid by 13 registers covering all models - 1923 to the present

* Spares and service scheme with associated discounts

* 80 area monthly meetings

* 12 Regional Centres covering the country

* 70 Overseas Associated Centres

* 2 exclusive insurance schemes

* 7 championships and RAC MSA affiliation

* 3 model-related rebuild seminars per year

To find out more about **THE MG CAR CLUB** please contact :

The MG Car Club Limited
Kimber House
PO Box 251
Abingdon
Oxon. OX14 1FF

Tel. 0235 555552
Fax. 0235 533755

THE ORIGINAL - AND STILL THE BEST

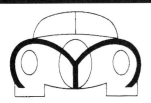
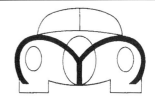

BROMSGROVE

CENTRE

THE MG SPECIALISTS.
MGB, V8, MGC, MIDGET
MGOC 5 STAR RECOMMENDED,
HERITAGE APPROVED

Through our involvement as specialists in the MGC market it was only natural that we should take an interest in the other big MG - the V8. Since the re-introduction of the MG Marque in the form of Rover's RV8 we have observed the interest in the V8 market grow progressively stronger and have built and converted many models to V8 specification for our customers. These conversions may be carried out to a customer's existing bodyshell or, as is becoming increasingly more popular with the availability of new shells, to a Heritage shell. One of our mechanics owns two V8's, one is an original GT and the other a Roadster which is being built onto a Heritage shell, and there are often lively exchanges between himself and Graham whenever the subject of V8 verses MGC is mentioned!

In addition to the extensive range of standard spares for MGB and V8 that we carry in stock we are now able to offer the following specialist parts for the V8 market.

- V8 Conversion steering racks.
- V8 Brake calipers (exchange or outright purchase).
- V8 Cross-drilled brake discs.
- V8 Tachometer and speedometer gauges.
- V8 3.07:1 ratio rear axles.
- V8 Clutch fork gaiters.
- V8 Washer bottle brackets.
- V8 Rear axle differential flanges.
- V8 Stainless steel exhaust systems.
- V8 Tubular manifolds.
- V8 Conversion propshafts.
- V8 Holley carburettors and Offenhauser inlet manifolds.

These services are also available to our customers.

- V8 Concours restorations.
- V8 GT and Roadster conversions.
- V8 Engine conversions to fast road specification (198 bhp at the rear wheels).
- V8 3.9 litre fuel injection conversions.
- V8 4.2 litre fuel injection conversions (available shortly).

IF YOU REQUIRE ANY SPARES FOR YOUR MG OR ARE INTERESTED IN ANY OF THE ITEMS THAT ARE LISTED ABOVE PLEASE DO NOT HESITATE TO CONTACT US.

FAST WORLDWIDE MAIL ORDER SERVICE

Unit 10, Sugarbrook Road, Aston Fields Industrial Estate,
Bromsgrove B61 3DW England.
Tel: Bromsgrove (0527) 879909 Fax: (0527) 575385